Biography of the autho

Alan Hunt CMG, FCIM, FRGS (UK) is a former Ambassador and Director of the University of Oxford Foreign Service Programme. His career in the British Diplomatic Service included postings in Tehran, Jedda, Panama, Madrid, Oslo, Buenos Aires (where he played a central role in the restoration of diplomatic relations after the Falklands conflict) and Düsseldorf (where he was Consul-General and Director-General for Trade and Investment Promotion in Germany). During postings in the Foreign and Commonwealth Office in London he handled international oil policy and relations with East Africa and Southern Europe, was Senior Civilian Directing Staff Member at the Royal College of Defence Studies and Director Overseas Trade. His final posting was as High Commissioner in Singapore. After leaving the Diplomatic Service he was for seven years Director of the Foreign Service Programme at Oxford University. He is now an author and consultant, in which capacity he also lectures on diplomacy and runs training courses in diplomatic practice. He is also a Visiting Professor at the College of Europe. He was made a CMG (Companion of the Order of St Michael and St George) in 1990 and is an Honorary Fellow of the Chartered Institute of Marketing and a Fellow of the Royal Geographical Society. Alan Hunt holds a First Class Honours Degree in European Studies from the University of East Anglia.

Acknowledgements

My thanks go to Rabih Haddad and Emily Fraser for their unstinting encouragement in the writing of this book, and to Evelyne de Mevius and her colleagues, Franz Thiel, Tomas Zak and Nancy Yacoub, for their rigorous and thoughtful editing: any errors or omissions are my responsibility, not theirs.

I am grateful also to the many practitioners and academics on whose writing and experience I have drawn while producing both this book and the UNITAR Course "Public Diplomacy in a Multipolar World". Their work is acknowledged in detail in the body of the book, but I reiterate my thanks to them here.

Finally, I must thank my wife, Meredith, whose constant understanding and support have been indispensable throughout my diplomatic and academic career.

Alan Hunt

PUBLIC DIPLOMACY
WHAT IT IS AND HOW TO DO IT

Alan Hunt

ISBN: 978-2-8399-1722-3

Published by the United Nations Institute for Training and Research (UNITAR).
Graphics and lay out by Franz Thiel.
Printed by Cointrin Copy Center.
Cover page: UNPhoto/MB

PUBLIC DIPLOMACY
WHAT IT IS AND HOW TO DO IT

Alan Hunt

United Nations Institute for Training and Research

Letter of the Executive Director of UNITAR

For the past 50 years, the United Nations Institute for Training and Research (UNITAR) has been developing capacities of individuals, organizations, and institutions to enhance global decision-making and support country-level action for shaping a better future.

Within UNITAR, the Multilateral Diplomacy Programme (MDP) provides capacity-building training to diplomats, international civil servants, and other government officials, alongside offering resources to strengthen their performance in multilateral working environments. After the *Glossary of Terms for UN delegates* in 2007, MDP published the *Manual for UN delegates* in 2011 and the *Practices of Diplomatic Protocol in Geneva* in 2015, all available in English and French.

It is in line with its mandate and constant endeavor to provide its beneficiaries with the most up-to-date and innovative tools that MDP is now releasing its most awaited brochure: *Public diplomacy. What it is and how to do it.*

Government endeavors to influence foreign publics have long pre-dated the concept of public diplomacy, coined in the 1960s. The communication and technology revolution that significantly shaped the 21st Century gave a powerful impetus to this particular way of conducting international relations. Governments lost their quasi monopoly on the control of information to the benefit of public opinion and non-state actors. Who, then, does public diplomacy belong to? How is the task divided? What are the responsibilities of government officials? What is the role of non-state actors? How to measure the power of the media?

Understanding the challenges posed by our ever-changing world is the core of UNITAR's vision. Processing and delivering the most up-to-date material for adapting to these changes lies at the heart of its mission. Alan Hunt's *Public diplomacy. What it is and how to do it* represents a major tool for diplomats around the world to perform effectively in their working environment, as well as being a must-have for anyone willing to explore this area in depth.

Nikhil Seth
United Nations Assistant Secretary-General
Executive Director
UNITAR

Table of contents

Chapter 3 | Related Activities: Nation Branding, Propaganda, Cultural Relations, Public Relations, Lobbying   31

Chapter 4 | Historical Development of Public Diplomacy   39

Chapter 5 | The Changing Global Environment   47

Chapter 6 | The Legal Framework for Public Diplomacy   55

Part 2 - Public Diplomacy - How to do it

Chapter 7 | Tools and Techniques of Public Diplomacy   61

Chapter 8 | Speech-making   67

Chapter 9 | Dealing with the Media   75

Chapter 10 | Use of Digital Technologies   83

Chapter 11 | Designing a Media Plan   91

Chapter 12 | How to be Interviewed 99

Chapter 13 | Public Diplomacy Campaigns 105

Chapter 14 | Evaluation 117

Part 3 - Conclusions

Chapter 15 | Key Lessons for Public Diplomacy Practitioners 127

Chapter 16 | Human Resources and Training Needs   135

Further Reading   139

Introduction

Many excellent books have been published on public diplomacy, the best of which offer powerful analysis and valuable strategic advice. While it is arguably invidious to select any one of these publications, Jan Melissen's *The New Public Diplomacy: Between Theory and Practice** is a seminal work, strongly recommended to anyone seeking an introduction to the world of public diplomacy. So too are Joseph Nye's books and articles on soft power. Special mention should also be made of the outstanding work conducted at the University of Southern California, where the Annenberg School is a rich repository of research and writing on public diplomacy. (Full details of these, and other relevant publications, can be found in the further reading section of this book.)

There are also many self-help books publicly available offering advice on generic skills such as speech-making and public relations management. Similarly, numerous foreign ministries also produce guidance on such techniques and on how to manage their particular public diplomacy programmes, such as scholarships and exchange programmes.

What seems to be lacking, however, is a book that seeks to combine both an analytical study of public diplomacy and advice on its day-to-day practice. This modest volume is an attempt to fill that gap.

Anyone familiar with UNITAR's online course "Public Diplomacy in a Multipolar World" will recognise much of the content of this book. In publishing the material in book form it is our hope that it will reach a much wider audience.

Alan Hunt, August 2015

---

* Jan Melissen (ed), *The New Public Diplomacy: Soft Power in International Relations*, Basingstoke, Palgrave Macmillan, 2005.

PART 1
PUBLIC DIPLOMACY -
WHAT IT IS

Chapter 1

Definitions of
Public Diplomacy

Elmer Davis, Director of the Office of War Information,
examines Nazi and Japanese propaganda organs
Library of Congress Prints & Photographs Division

1.1 Introduction

Public diplomacy is regarded as a widely accepted concept, although it is much debated, both in theory and in practice.

In this chapter, we shall consider the origin of the term "public diplomacy"; some alternative definitions; the relevance of communications theory; the distinction between traditional and public diplomacy; the three essential dimensions of public diplomacy; and the question of listening and messaging.

1.2 Origin of the term "public diplomacy"

The term "public diplomacy" in its current use[1] was coined in 1965, at the height of the Cold War, by the American academic and former diplomat Edmund Gullion. The United States was engaged, with its allies, in an ideological struggle with the Soviet Union, entailing strenuous efforts by governments on both sides to demonstrate to the public in each others' countries – and elsewhere in the world – the superiority of their cause. Gullion was seeking a means of describing the activities undertaken by the United States to persuade and influence people that would distinguish them from those of the Soviet Union, which were regarded in the West as propaganda. (We shall look more closely at propaganda in Chapter 3.)

Although closely associated with the activities of the United States Government – both during the Cold War and after 9/11 – the term "public diplomacy" has now become an accepted description of public information activities undertaken by governments and, some would argue, by other international actors as well. The adoption of the term did not itself change these activities, many of which had been in existence for a long time. In recent decades, however, public diplomacy practices have evolved rapidly, reflecting technological and societal change. In response to this evolution, reference is now frequently made to the "new public diplomacy"[2].

1.3 Some alternative definitions

As with diplomacy more broadly, there is no shortage of definitions of public diplomacy.
When Edmund Gullion set up the Edward R. Murrow Center of Public Diplomacy in 1965, the new institution's brochure described public diplomacy as follows:

> *"Public diplomacy... deals with the influence of public attitudes on the formation and execution of foreign policies. It encompasses dimensions of international relations beyond traditional diplomacy; the cultivation by governments of public opinion in other countries; the interaction of private groups and interests in one country with another; the reporting of foreign affairs and its impact*

---

1   The earliest recorded use of the phrase «public diplomacy» was in 1856 in a leading article in The Times. The intended meaning of the phrase was not however that current today. At the time, the expression was used as a synonym for "civility" in a piece criticizing the public behaviour of the then United States President Franklin Pierce. Subsequently, the term was used to refer to public declarations made by governments, or for the open diplomacy expounded in, for example, President Woodrow Wilson's Fourteen Points. (See Nicholas J. Cull, *'Public Diplomacy' before Gullion: The Evolution of a Phrase*, University of Southern California Center on Public Diplomacy, 18 April, 2006.)
2   See, for example, Jan Melissen (ed), *The New Public Diplomacy: Soft Power in International Relations*, Basingstoke, Palgrave Macmillan, 2005.

on policy; communication between those whose job is communication, as diplomats and foreign correspondents; and the process of intercultural communications." [3]

In 1987, the United States State Department put it more baldly:

"Public Diplomacy refers to government-sponsored programs intended to inform or influence public opinion in other countries; its chief instruments are publications, motion pictures, cultural exchanges, radio and television." [4]

In 1990, Hans Tuch, another former American diplomat, offered a more considered view:

"[Public diplomacy] is a government's process of communicating with foreign publics in an attempt to bring about understanding of its nation's ideas, its institutions and culture, as well as its national goals and policies." [5]

The notion that receptiveness as well as transmission is entailed in such communication is suggested in the definition employed when the once autonomous United States Information Agency (USIA) was merged into the State Department:

"Public Diplomacy seeks to promote the national interest of the United States through understanding, informing, and influencing foreign audiences." [6]

Recent commentators[7] have objected to definitions that are exclusively focused on action by governments – a criticism it is worth noting does not apply to Gullion's original definition – when there is a range of international actors, including international organisations and non-governmental organisations (NGOs), engaged in activities related to public diplomacy today. Irrespective of the debate about definition – on which, see also the discussion below about diplomacy more generally –, most governments practising public diplomacy are in no doubt that to be successful they must collaborate with a wide variety of partners and engage in genuine conversations with their respective audiences.

A colourful view of American efforts to influence foreign publics was advanced by the late Richard Holbrooke, until his death President Obama's civilian adviser on Afghanistan and Pakistan:

"Call it public diplomacy, call it public affairs, psychological warfare, if you really want to be blunt, propaganda." [8]

As we shall see in Chapter 3, there is in fact a distinction to be drawn between public diplomacy and propaganda, even though in both cases the object is broadly the same: to get people to think and behave in ways conducive to one's own interests.

3   See Nicholas J. Cull, 2006.
4   US Department of State, *Dictionary of International Relations Terms*, 1987.
5   Hans Tuch, *Communicating with the World: US Public Diplomacy Overseas*, New York, St Martin's Press, 1990.
6   Planning Group for Integration of USIA into the Dept. of State, June 1997.
7   See e.g., Jan Melissen (ed), 2005.
8   Richard Holbrooke, *Get the Message Out*, Washington Post, 28 October, 2001.

1.4 The relevance of communication theory

In a 2008 review of the human resources dimension of American public diplomacy[9], the United States Advisory Commission on Public Diplomacy bemoaned, inter alia, the absence of training in communication theory for public diplomacy practitioners. The Commission recommended that this lacuna be addressed, with particular emphasis on political communication/rhetoric, advertising/marketing theory and public opinion analysis.

Understanding audiences is key to devising the best means of influencing them. How might knowledge of communication theory help achieve this?

In their book *Applying Communication Theory for Professional Life*[10], Marianne Dainton and Elaine D. Zelley distinguish between what they call the "every-day view" of communication (i.e. the flow of information from one person to another) and the prevailing scholarly definition of communication (i.e. the process by which people interactively create, sustain and manage meaning).

Dainton and Zelley describe a communication theory as any systemic summary about the nature of the communication process. They distinguish between common-sense theory (which may have no objective basis), working theory (based on professional experience) and scholarly theory (based on detailed research). They discuss the characteristics and relative merits of the four broad categories of research on which the latter rests: experiment, survey, textual analysis and ethnography, which typically involves immersion of the researcher into a particular culture or context. They also support the view that communication competence is best understood as a balance between effectiveness (achieving one's goals) and appropriateness (acting in accordance with social expectations).

Helpful as this starting point is, the public diplomacy practitioner seeking relevant guidance is nevertheless confronted with a vast and complex landscape of theories of communication from which to choose. In a bid to render this terrain more navigable, E. M. Griffin, in his book *A First Look at Communication Theory*[11], describes Robert Craig's seven established traditions of communication theory as follows:

i.   Socio-psychological (interpersonal interaction and influence);
ii.   Cybernetic (a system of information processing);
iii.   Rhetorical (artful public address);
iv.   Semiotic (the process of sharing meaning through signs);
v.   Socio-cultural (the creation and enactment of social reality);
vi.   Critical (a reflective challenge of unjust discourse);
vii.   Phenomenological (the experience of self and others through dialogue).

---

9   *Getting the People Part Right: A Report on the Human Resources Dimension of US Public Diplomacy*, United States Advisory Commission on Public Diplomacy, 2008.
10   Marianne Dainton and Elaine D. Zelley, *Applying Communication Theory for Professional Life*, 2nd edition, New York Sage Publications Inc, 2011.
11   Em Griffin, *A First look at Communication Theory*, 8th edition, New York, McGraw Hill, 2011.

Quoting as an example the National Communication Association (NCA)'s 1999 *Credo for Ethical Communication*[12] – which calls for, inter alia, truthfulness, accuracy, honesty and reason; acceptance of responsibility for the consequences of communication; and understanding of other communicators – Griffin adds to Craig's list a further tradition, namely:

viii. Ethical (interaction between people of character in just and beneficial ways).

There is undoubtedly material of interest to be mined in all these traditions (as an obvious example, some trainers in public speaking employ Aristotle's *Rhetoric* as a basis for their teaching), but it remains a formidable body of work to explore. Griffin has however distilled from this multiplicity of theories what he describes as ten recurring principles:

i. Motivation: there is a social need for affiliation, achievement and control; and a strong desire to reduce uncertainty and anxiety;

ii. Self-image: communication affects, and is affected by one's sense of identity, which is strongly shaped within the context of one's culture;

iii. Credibility: verbal and non-verbal messages are validated or discounted by others' perception of one's competence and character;

iv. Expectation: what one expects to hear and see will affect one's perception, interpretation and response during an interaction;

v. Audience adaptation: by mindfully creating a person-centred message specific to the situation, one increases the possibility of achieving one's communication goals (but too much adaptation may mean losing the authenticity of the message or the integrity of one's own beliefs);

vi. Social construction: persons in conversation co-construct their own social realities and are simultaneously shaped by the worlds they co-create;

vii. Shared meaning: communication is successful to the extent to which a common interpretation is shared of the signs used.

viii. Narrative: people respond favourably to stories and dramatic images with which they can identify;

ix. Conflict: Unjust communication stifles needed conflict; healthy communication can make conflict productive;

x. Dialogue: Transparent conversation often creates unanticipated outcomes arising from the parties' respect for disparate voices.[13]

Dainton and Zelley offer a somewhat different synthesis of thirteen important variables that influence the communication process: cohesion, connection and in-groups; context; expectations; face and self versus other orientation; individual qualities; interest and involvement; needs; power and control; relationship; rewards; rules; uncertainty and ambiguity; and values and beliefs. While they make the point that professional communicators should be guided by individual theories as relevant, they conclude with the following general insight:

"If we were to summarize the single biggest piece of advice culled from all the theories ... it would be that competent communicators are those who take a receiver orientation to communication; in pursuit of their own goals they consider what others need to hear (and how they might hear it) so that they might accomplish their goals." [14]

---

12   The full text of the NCA's credo, published in 1999, can be found at their website: http://www.natcom.org/uploadedFiles/About_NCA/Leadership_and_Governance/Public_Policy_Platform/PDF-PolicyPlatform-NCA_Credo_for_Ethical_Communication.pdf (Retrieved August 2015).
13   Em Griffin, 2011.
14   Marianne Dainton and Elaine D. Zelley, 2011.

1.5 Comparison between traditional diplomacy and public diplomacy

Leaving aside the non-technical description of diplomacy as the exercise of tact and courtesy[15], most conventional definitions conceive of diplomacy as a mechanism for managing relations between states. In 1939, in his classic work Diplomacy, Sir Harold Nicolson selectively adopted the following section of the definition then in use by the Oxford English Dictionary:

> "...the management of international relations by negotiation, the method by which these relations are adjusted and managed by ambassadors and envoys; the business or art of the diplomatist." [16]

A more recent definition by exclusion is offered by G. R. Berridge:

> "[Diplomacy's] chief purpose is to enable states to secure the objectives of foreign policy without resort to force, propaganda or law." [17]

Both these definitions are clearly rooted in the nation state system of today's world. In an attempt to construct a general theory of diplomacy that might apply in all places and at all times, C. Jönsson and M. Hall have argued that diplomacy is an institution that structures relations between polities (i.e., not necessarily between nation states as currently understood). Its practitioners have a shared language and conventions; and they have mutual expectations and rules (reciprocity, precedence and diplomatic immunity). Diplomacy's three fundamental functions are communication, representation and reproduction of international society.[18]

Others go further, arguing that, already in today's world, states no longer have a monopoly on diplomacy. Melissen, for example, describes diplomacy as:

> "...the mechanism of representation, communication and negotiation through which states and other international actors conduct their business." [19]

Raymond Saner, of Diplomacy Dialogue, believes that multinational corporations (MNCs) and civil societies are practising diplomacy alongside traditional diplomats:

> "Diplomacy has ... broadened to include states and non-state actors.....diplomacy has become the continuation of politics, economics and business by other means." [20]

A professional diplomat, basing his position on the traditional conception of diplomacy, might object to this latter claim, arguing that non-state actors cannot, by definition, be practising diplomacy: however similar their activities may be to diplomacy, they are in fact engaged in negotiation more broadly defined, or in lobbying or public relations. Those arguing for a less restrictive definition of diplomacy would respond that this traditionalist position simply ignores the radical changes taking place in international society.

15   See, for example: "Diplomacy is to do and say The nastiest things in the nicest way.", Isaac Goldberg, *The Reflex*, October 1927.
16   Harold Nicolson, *Diplomacy*, originally published 1939, 3rd edition, Oxford University Press, 1970.
17   G. R. Berridge, *Diplomacy – Theory and Practice*, 3rd edition, Palgrave Macmillan, 2005.
18   C. Jönsson and M. Hall, *Essence of Diplomacy*, Palgrave Macmillan, 2005.
19   Jan Melissen (ed), *Innovation in Diplomatic Practice*, Palgrave Macmillan, 1999.
20   Raymond Saner, *Diplomacy Dialogue*, in his presentation Postmodern Economic Diplomacy, during a symposium entitled "*Challenges Facing the 21st Century Diplomat: Representation, Communication, Negotiation and Training*" organised by the College of Europe in Bruges, 25-26 October 2011.

Using conventional definitions of diplomacy, it is possible to determine without difficulty the distinction between traditional and public diplomacy: the former is concerned principally with governments influencing governments, the latter with governments influencing publics. Using the more inclusive definitions of Melissen and Saner somewhat clouds the picture – which, they would argue, offers an accurate depiction of the fuzzy world of postmodern transnational relations, in which most actors are not as much in control of events as they would wish.[21]

1.6 The three dimensions of public diplomacy

One possible way of mitigating the difference between the traditionalists and those who argue for a more flexible interpretation of diplomacy is to consider separately the three dimensions of public diplomacy identified by Joseph Nye (whose concept of soft power we shall be looking at in Chapter 2).[22]

Nye asserts that all three dimensions of public diplomacy are important, and that they require different relative proportions of direct government information and long-term cultural relationships.

The first and most immediate dimension is daily communication, which involves explaining the context of domestic and foreign policy decisions to both the domestic and international press. The day-to-day dimension also involves preparation for dealing with crises and having a rapid response capability for countering false charges or misleading information.

The second dimension identified by Nye is strategic communication (i.e. public diplomacy campaigns), in which a set of simple themes is developed, focusing on particular policy initiatives, much as in a political or advertising campaign. The campaign plans symbolic events and communications over the course of a set period to reinforce the central themes, or to advance a particular government policy.[23]

Nye's third stage of public diplomacy is the development of lasting relationships with key individuals over many years through scholarships, exchanges, training, seminars, conferences, and access to media channels. It is here – although not exclusively so – that there is clearly the greatest scope for involvement by non-state actors, even if – as Nye argues – an element of state funding is desirable.

Each of these three dimensions of public diplomacy plays an important role in helping to create an attractive image of a country that can improve its prospects for obtaining its desired outcomes. But, as Nye stresses, even the best advertising cannot sell an unpopular product: a communications strategy cannot work if it cuts against the grain of policy. Actions speak louder than words: public diplomacy as mere window dressing for hard power projection is unlikely to succeed. Policy and diplomacy must match – and effective public diplomacy is a two-way street that involves listening as well as talking.[24]

21   Jan Melissen (ed), 2005.
22   Joseph S. Nye Jr., *Soft Power: The Means to Success in World Politics*, New York, Public Affairs, 2004.
23   The example Nye quotes is the public diplomacy action that accompanied the implementation of NATO's two-track decision to deploy missiles in Western Europe, while negotiating to remove existing Soviet intermediate range missiles. The Soviet Union launched a concerted campaign to influence European opinion and make the deployment impossible. The United States' response stressed the multilateral nature of the NATO decision, encouraged European governments to take the lead when possible, and used non-governmental American participants to counter Soviet arguments.
24   Joseph S. Nye Jr., 2004.

1.7 Listening and messaging

To illustrate this last point, Ali Fisher and Aurélie Bröckerhoff have suggested the following spectrum of public diplomacy modes, running from listening at one end to messaging at the other:

LISTENING
Listening shows respect and it may sometimes actually change behaviour. But it must be genuine: and, on its own, it is limited in scope.

FACILITATION
Facilitation entails helping others to achieve their goals, for example Norway's efforts to advance the MEPP.

BUILDING NETWORKS or LONG-TERM RELATIONSHIPS
This is the process of identifying and cultivating people likely to be of influence in the future: it offers no immediate return.

CULTURAL EXCHANGE
This is a reciprocal activity.

CULTURAL DIPLOMACY
This is moving towards messaging, i.e. "telling a story".

BROADCASTING
By definition, broadcasting entails, above all, transmitting, although there will not necessarily be direct government messaging involved if the broadcaster enjoys editorial independence.

DIRECT MESSAGING (TELLING)
At this end of the spectrum lie nation branding, tourism promotion, policy advocacy and information correction.[25]

1.8 Conclusions

The essential component of public diplomacy, seeking to influence foreign publics, long pre-dates the existence of the term itself. There is a spectrum of public diplomacy modes ranging from "listening" at one end to "telling" at the other: and listening is the key to effective communication. Public diplomacy has three dimensions: daily communication; campaigns (Joseph Nye's "strategic communication"); and the development of lasting relationships. No public diplomacy will be effective if it is not aligned with actual policy and behaviour. Public diplomacy today is largely informed by Nye's concept of "soft power". We shall look at this concept in Chapter 2.

---

25   Ali Fisher and Aurélie Bröckerhoff, *Options for Influence*, Berkeley, Counterpoint, 2008.

Chapter 2

THE MEANS
TO SUCCESS
IN WORLD
POLITICS

JOSEPH S. NYE, Jr.

Soft Power

Joseph Nye - Chatham House, 2011

2.1 Introduction

The expression "soft power" is so widely used – and frequently misused – as to have become almost a cliché. It is nevertheless a useful concept, which helps to inform an understanding of public diplomacy. In this lesson we shall look at how the term came into being, consider the relative merits of hard and soft power, and discuss the impact of the concept of soft power on the practice of diplomacy.

2.2 Joseph Nye's concept of soft power

Joseph Nye was Dean of the John F. Kennedy School of Government at Harvard University from 1995 to 2004. His previous career had taken him from being Director of the Center for International Affairs at Harvard to a series of posts in Washington, including Deputy to the Under Secretary of State for Security Assistance, Science and Technology; Chairman of the National Intelligence Council and, from 1994 to 1995, Assistant Secretary of Defense for International Security Affairs.

In 1990, Nye wrote a book entitled *Bound to Lead: The Changing Nature of American Power*[26], in which he coined the term "soft power" to describe the assets of the United States in its international dealings other than the traditional ones of military and economic power. Nye's aim was in part to counter arguments that America was in decline. When he returned to the idea of soft power in a 2001 book, *The Paradox of American Power: Why the World's Only Superpower Can't Go It Alone*[27], it was, however, this time to counsel against American triumphalism and to advocate multilateralism. In due course, in 2004, Nye wrote his classic work, *Soft Power: The Means to Success in World Politics*.[28]

Nye's starting point in Soft Power was that the true nature of power was difficult to understand:

> *"Power is like the weather. Everyone depends on it and talks about it, but few understand it...Power is also like love, easier to experience than to define or measure, but no less real for that."* [29]

Nye argued that in the international realm there were essentially three sources of power:

> *"...Power is the ability to influence the behaviour of others to get the outcomes one wants. But there are several ways to affect the behaviour of others. You can coerce them with threats; you can induce them with payments; or you can attract and co-opt them to want what you want."* [30]

26   Joseph S. Nye Jr., *Bound to Lead: The Changing Nature of American Power*, New York, Simon and Schuster, 1990.
27   Joseph S. Nye Jr., *The Paradox of American Power: Why the World's Only Superpower can't Go It Alone*, Oxford University Press, 2001.
28   Joseph S. Nye Jr., *Soft Power: The Means to Success in World Politics*, New York, Public Affairs, 2004.
29   *Ibid.*
30   *Ibid.*

Writing against the background of American military operations in Iraq and Afghanistan, Nye sought to demonstrate that military and economic power alone could not achieve a state's international ambitions:

> "A country may obtain the outcomes it wants in world politics because other countries, – admiring its values, emulating its example, aspiring to its level of prosperity and openness – want to follow it. In this sense it is also important to set the agenda and attract others in world politics, and not only to force them to change by threatening military force or economic sanctions. This soft power – getting others to want the outcomes that you want – co-opts people rather than coercing them." [31]

Nye was at pains to distinguish soft power from influence, which could be exercised through the hard power of threats or inducements. He also emphasised that soft power was, in general, more difficult to deploy than hard power:

> "Soft power is more difficult, because many of its crucial resources are outside the control of governments, and their effects depend heavily on acceptance by the receiving audiences. Moreover, soft power resources often work indirectly by shaping the environment for policy, and sometimes take years to produce the desired outcomes... Generally, soft-power resources are slower, more diffuse, and more cumbersome to wield than hard-power resources." [32]

In his more recent writing, Nye has bemoaned the continuing United States neglect of its soft power resources, which he sees as leading to a decline in America's image and influence in the world. [33]

While power itself – and soft power in particular – may be, as Nye suggests, difficult to measure, this has not prevented attempts to measure the resources that contribute to a nation's soft power (i.e. their potential for influence). These have tended to be based on public opinion surveys, but in 2013 the Institute for Government in the UK published, for the third year running, a soft power index ranking a range of selected countries (forty in the index for 2012). [34] The ranking was based on five objective criteria: culture, government, diplomacy, education and business (which together accounted for 70% of the index weighting) [35] in combination with seven subjective metrics: design/architecture (a new category for 2012), cultural output, global leadership, soft power icons, cuisine, national airline/major airport and commercial brands (which accounted for the remaining 30%). Despite Nye's concern about the neglect of its soft power resources, the United States, with particularly strong scores in the culture and education sub-indices, was ranked number two in the 2012 IfG index, behind the United Kingdom. Subsequent league tables published by the IfG's partner, Monocle Magazine, placed Germany in first place in 2013 and the United States in first place in 2014. [36]

31   *Ibid.*
32   *Ibid.*
33   Joseph S. Nye Jr., *The War on Soft Power*, Foreign Policy, 12 April 2011. http://www.foreignpolicy.com/articles/2011/04/12/the_war_on_soft_power (Retrieved August 2015).
34   Jonathan McClory, *The New Persuaders III: A 2012 Global Ranking of Soft Power*, Institute for Government, 2013: http://www.instituteforgovernment.org.uk/sites/default/files/publications/The%20new%20persuaders%20III_0.pdf (Retrieved August 2015).
35   These criteria are an expanded version of the three primary sources of soft power identified by Nye: culture, political values and foreign policy (Joseph S. Nye Jr., 2004). Taken in conjunction with the subjective metrics, they are also broadly consistent with the six sub-brands identified by Simon Anholt in discussion of nation branding, namely: exports; governance; culture and heritage; people; tourism; and investment and immigration (See Chapter 3).
36   http://monocle.com/magazine/ (Retrieved August 2015).

2.3 The relative value of hard and soft power

Joseph Stalin is reported to have said: "The Pope? How many divisions has he got?"[37], leaving little doubt as to his own view of the true source of power. In the early study of international relations, power was treated as a realist concept, its sources measured, relatively straightforwardly, by tangible components such as military capacity, population, territory, natural resources and economic performance. With the evolution of international relations studies, competing schools of thoughts have challenged the realist perspective. While the nature of power remains contested, there now seems to be general acceptance of the two categories of "hard" and "soft" power, even though there may be disagreement about their relative value.[38]

There are striking examples in relatively recent history of superior hard power not prevailing, one of the most notable of which, quoted by Nye, is the Vietnam War. There are also examples of hard power being successfully exerted, but at a considerable cost to a country's soft power: for example, the Soviet Union's suppression of the uprisings in Hungary in 1956 and Czechoslovakia in 1968, and the United States military intervention in Iraq in 2003. Examples of soft power success disproportionate to hard power capacity are Norway, which has carved out a notable niche for itself as a facilitator of peace in third countries, and – despite Stalin's mockery – the Vatican.[39]

Nye has never claimed (as some students of international relations seem tempted to believe) that soft power could supersede hard power. On the contrary, he is an advocate of a strong defence capability. However, he advises against exclusive dependence on hard power in an age of virtually instant communication and social networks, when public opinion is increasingly important in influencing the policies adopted by governments (for reasons to be examined in Chapter 5 below). What Nye advocates is "smart power", of which he says:

> "Smart power is neither hard nor soft. It is both." [40]

2.4 The impact of the concept of soft power on the practice of diplomacy

Just as public diplomacy, although otherwise described, was practised long before it acquired its name in the 1960s, soft power did not suddenly come into being as a result of Nye's theoretical construction. Confucius advised that emperors should attract by their virtue[41], which is a concise summation of Nye's central insight. Nye himself quotes examples from history of the exercise of soft power by leaders such as Richelieu and Louis XIV (see also Chapter 4 below).[42]

---

37   Quoted in Winston Churchill, *The Second World War*, 1948.
38   Jonathan McClory, *The New Persuaders II: A 2011 Global Ranking of Soft Power*, Institute for Government, 2011: http://www.instituteforgovernment.org.uk/publications/new-persuaders-ii (Retrieved August 2015).
39   Joseph S. Nye Jr., 2004.
40   *Ibid.*
41   "It is for this reason that, when distant subjects are not submissive, one cultivates one's moral quality in order to attract them." *The Analects of Confucius*, Book XVI.
42   Joseph S. Nye Jr., 2004.

Nye's concept has nevertheless had an impact on the practice of diplomacy. His ideas have been widely absorbed into the conventional wisdom of foreign ministries, and governments have made strenuous efforts – not always well-guided – to harness their country's soft power in pursuit of their objectives.

Some observers have detected in this scramble by governments to commit themselves to soft power approaches "an overwhelming sense of enthusiasm outpacing competence", with policy makers running the risk of trying to use their soft power before they have actually identified it.[43]

A further impetus to favouring soft power has come from the fiscal consolidation facing many countries in the West as a result of the global financial crisis. Foreign and defence ministry budgets have been cut and governments have turned to soft power tools – in particular those not state-financed – to achieve foreign policy objectives. On the other hand, budget constraints have also had an impact on public diplomacy expenditure, as Nye has observed is the case in the United States. Countries like China and India, however, are devoting increasing resources in this field.[44]

2.5 Conclusions

The exercise of soft power is getting others to want the outcomes you want by co-opting them rather than coercing or bribing them. Exclusive dependence on hard power is less effective in an age when public opinion is increasingly important in influencing government policies. Soft power is not a substitute for hard power, but in judicious combination with the latter it constitutes what Nye describes as "smart power".

---

43   Jonathan McClory, 2011.
44   *Ibid.*

Public Diplomacy: What it is - and how to do it

Chapter 3

Related Activities: Nation Branding, Propaganda, Cultural Relations, Public Relations, Lobbying

Flags of member nations flying at United Nations Headquarters
UN Photo/Joao Araujo Pinto

3.1 Introduction

As we have seen in Chapter 1, there is much discussion as to the precise definition of public diplomacy, a concept that is in any case in a state of evolution. In this chapter we shall examine a number of related activities: nation branding, propaganda, cultural relations, public relations, and lobbying. In an attempt to distinguish these activities from public diplomacy, we shall hope to cast more light on public diplomacy itself.

3.2 Nation branding

Conflicting claims are made about nation-branding and public diplomacy: that they are the same thing; that they are different things; and that each is a subset of the other.

While their activities are undoubtedly closely allied, it is fair to say that nation – or place – branding as a concept is both newer and more ambitious than public diplomacy, whose objectives tend to be specific and limited and whose practitioners by and large recognise that the impact they have is marginal.[45, 46] Those who seek to brand a nation, by contrast, are faced with an immense and complex task.

Brands are by origin a commercial marketing concept. While there are principles of marketing that are relevant to public diplomacy – including above all the need to understand the customer –, it is an enormous leap of faith to believe that a country can be branded in much the same way as a motor car or breakfast cereal.

The main difficulty about applying commercial marketing to nation-branding is that the fundamental rule of marketing is to say one thing very clearly about the product being marketed. A country, however, is a complicated entity and has many different sub-brands deriving from the experiences of foreigners in different fields. The acknowledged guru in the field, Simon Anholt, has devised the following categories for measuring the strength of a country's brand:

i. Exports: Determines the public's image of products and services from each country and the extent to which consumers proactively seek or avoid products from each country-of-origin;
ii. Governance: Measures public opinion regarding the level of national government competency and fairness; and describes individuals' beliefs about each country's government, as well as its perceived commitment to global issues such as democracy, justice, poverty and the environment;
iii. Culture and Heritage: Reveals global perceptions of each nation's heritage and appreciation for its contemporary culture, including film, music, art, sport and literature;
iv. People: Measures the population's reputation for competence, education, openness and friendliness and other qualities, as well as perceived levels of potential hostility and discrimination;

---

45   Jan Melissen (ed), 2005.
46   Alan K. Henrikson, *What Can Public Diplomacy Achieve? Discussion Papers in Diplomacy*, Netherlands Institute of International Relations "Clingendael", 2006: http://www.clingendael.nl/sites/default/files/What-can-public-diplomacy-achieve.pdf (Retrieved August 2015).

v.   Tourism: Captures the level of interest in visiting a country and the draw of natural and man-made tourist attractions;

vi.   Investment and Immigration: Determines the power to attract people to live, work, or study in each country and reveals how people perceive a country's economic and social situation.[47]

Identifying a single brand to embrace all these categories is extremely difficult, not least because the experience of foreigners in many of the categories is outside the control of any government, however well coordinated the branding exercise may be. It is also arguably counter-productive to attempt to reduce to a single brand a richly complex and diverse identity – whose very diversity may be the essence of its attraction.

Anholt has suggested that one way of squaring this circle is to have a striking overarching theme to act as a signpost, allowing for more detailed exposition of the brand once the target audience's attention has been attracted. The danger he identifies in this approach is that governments may simply adopt catchy slogans devised by public relations companies, which have little of substance behind them.[48]

Anholt also draws a clear distinction between the observation that countries have brand images – a useful metaphor – and the assertion that a country can be branded, which he describes as an "excessively ambitious, entirely unproven and ultimately irresponsible claim". Brand image can be managed, and over time improved, but success in this endeavour rests on developing good policies that clearly resonate with a country's values and beliefs. The image can only be earned; it cannot be constructed or invented.[49] Who a nation is (identity) determines how it acts (behaviour); and how it acts determines how it is perceived.[50]

Re-branding is particularly difficult for large, powerful, well-known nations, whose brand – for good or ill – is already strong and who are in any case judged largely by their actions on the world stage. Smaller, less well-known countries stand a better chance of projecting their chosen image, provided it is consistent with the true nature of the country: as we have seen in discussion of soft power in Chapter 2, a new label will not sell an inferior product. The problem for smaller nations is one of resources, although the Internet offers many possibilities for cost-effective action. This need not include large amounts of expensive advertising, which is arguably relevant only to the harder-selling elements of a nation's brand, such as tourism or inward investment (what Anholt describes as "destination branding").[51, 52]

There have been some notable successes in positive management of brand image, as for example in Spain, after the death of Franco, when the country underwent a genuine transition.[53]

---

47   Simon Anholt, *The Anholt-GfK Roper Nations Brand Index*, 2009 : http://www.simonanholt.com/Research/research-the-anholt-gfk-roper-nation-brands-index-sm.aspx (Retrieved August 2015).

48   Simon Anholt, *Should place brands be simple?*, Place Branding and Public Diplomacy, 2009, Volume 5, Number 1: http://www.simonanholt.com/Publications/publications-other-articles.aspx (Retrieved August 2015).

49   Simon Anholt, *Place branding – is it marketing or isn't it ?*, Place Branding and Public Diplomacy, 2007, Volume 4, Number 1: http://www.simonanholt.com/Publications/publications-other-articles.aspx (Retrieved August 2015).

50   Simon Anholt, 2009.

51   Simon Anholt, *"Nation Branding" in Asia*, Place Branding and Public Diplomacy, 2008, Volume 4, Number 4: http://www.simonanholt.com/Publications/publications-other-articles.aspx (Retrieved August 2015).

52   For a concise encapsulation of Anholt's views on nation-branding, see *Endnote to Public Diplomacy Magazine*, University of Southern California, Summer, 2009: http://www.simonanholt.com/Publications/publications-other-articles.aspx (Retrieved August.2015).

53   For an account of the Spanish re-branding experience, see Fiona Gilmore, *A country – can it be repositioned? Spain – the success story of country branding*, The Journal of Brand Management, April 2002, Volume 9, Number 4-5: https://placebrandingofpublicspace.files.wordpress.com/2013/01/a-country-spain_gilmore.pdf (Retrieved August 2015).

3.3 Propaganda

There are those who see no distinction between propaganda and public diplomacy, and contend that the latter is simply what we used to call the former. Advocates of the "new" public diplomacy argue that each have clearly distinctive features.

Let us begin by considering the origin of the word "propaganda".

In the 17th Century, Pope Gregory XV established the Sacred Congregation for the Propagation of the Faith, whose function was to disseminate the Catholic faith. In due course, the word "propaganda" (from the Latin "propagare", to spread) came into use more widely. It was originally a neutral term that meant using largely factual and accurate information to advance whatever cause one was promoting.

In the First World War the German Government began to distort the meaning of propaganda by spreading information that was not accurate, to which the Allies responded in kind. This process was carried to the ultimate by Goebbels in the Second World War, with the conception of the "big lie", i.e. a gross distortion of the truth, repeated continuously until it came to be believed.[54] The Soviet Union developed propaganda on similar lines.

A succinct definition of propaganda is to be found in the following extract from a secret British Political Warfare Executive document dated 1942:

> "Propaganda ... is the deliberate direction, or even manipulation, of information to secure a definite objective. It is an attempt to direct the thinking of the recipient, without his conscious collaboration, into predetermined channels. It is the conditioning of the recipient by devious methods with an ulterior motive. Propaganda emphasises those facts which best serve its purpose. It creates the atmosphere in which the audience is most susceptible to suggestion. By power of suggestion, which in favourable circumstances becomes instruction, it secures positive action." [55]

It is virtually impossible today to divorce the term "propaganda" from the excesses of the Nazi and Soviet periods. This was why, as we saw in Chapter 1, Gullion was determined to find a new description for United States information activity during the Cold War.

It is also difficult today for states to base propaganda on lies. The speed with which information is disseminated globally through independent networks is such that governments are rapidly caught out if they seek to fly in the face of the truth.

But, even adhering to the most benign conception of propaganda, namely that it always deploys the truth – albeit selectively –, there is an argument for saying that it is not public diplomacy as currently understood. Propaganda is about narrowing down the perceptions of the target audience, i.e. closing their minds to any alternative possibilities. Public diplomacy – the "new" public diplomacy – is much more about generating creative dialogue.[56] While public diplomacy and propaganda may have common roots in history, and unarguably share the broad aims of seeking to influence foreign publics, they sit at different points on the continuum of persuasion. In real life, this does not prevent governments – perhaps unwittingly – from engaging in both propaganda and public diplomacy simultaneously.

54   Richard O'Halloran, *Strategic Communication*, Parameters, Carlisle, US Army War College, Autumn 2007, pp. 4-14: http://strategicstudiesin-stitute.army.mil/pubs/parameters/Articles/07autumn/halloran.pdf (Retrieved August 2015).
55   British Political Warfare Executive, *The Meaning, Techniques and Methods of Political Warfare*, 1942.
56   Jan Melissen (ed), 2005.

3.4 Cultural relations

If propaganda sits at one end of the continuum of persuasion, cultural relations, which are in themselves devoid of any overt message, sit at the other.

Cultural relations between nations enjoy a long history, much of it independent of government activity. For many involved in academic and artistic exchange, there is an intrinsic value to such exchange going beyond government objectives in the international realm.

Governments nevertheless encourage cultural relations – and by exploiting them convert them into "cultural diplomacy" – in the belief that they do in fact serve their own purposes. Although it is difficult to measure the effect, proponents of cultural relations as a component of public diplomacy argue that consistent, mutual cultural exchange over time creates an environment where respect and tolerance flourish, leading in turn to increased trade in skills, knowledge, products, capital and people. Anholt suggests that cultural relations are one of the few demonstrably effective forms of place branding because they offer some pleasure in return for the consumer's attention; and that, for example, educational support programmes in foreign schools are often an effective way of enhancing a nation's image.[57, 58]

As we have seen, public diplomacy practitioners tend to see cultural relations as part of their portfolio and to think in terms of cultural diplomacy. This view of cultural relations is embodied in a State Department report of 2005, entitled "Cultural Diplomacy – the Linchpin of Public Diplomacy" and is rooted in the role played by American popular culture during the Cold War in the defeat of Communism in the Soviet Union.[59] In this document, cultural diplomacy is defined, drawing on an earlier report by the Washington Center for Arts and Culture as:

> " ...the exchange of ideas, information, art, and other aspects of culture among nations and their peoples in order to foster mutual understanding." [60]

A somewhat more nuanced view is argued by the United Kingdom think tank Demos in a paper entitled "Cultural Diplomacy", published in 2007. While calling for greater resources and a more strategic and systematic approach to UK cultural diplomacy, the authors are opposed to the use of culture as a tool of public diplomacy. They argue that the value of cultural activity comes from its independence and from the fact that it represents and connects people, rather than having to do with governments or policy.[61]

There is clearly potential for tension between those involved in cultural relations – who aspire to maximum autonomy in order to maintain credibility – and those whose responsibility it is to achieve foreign policy objectives – who seek closer coordination of overseas cultural activities. Countries with

57   Simon Anholt, 2009.
58   This view is shared by, for example, the German Government, whose cultural relations and education policy ("Winning Hearts and Minds for Germany and Forging Lasting Networks") includes support for more than 1,500 partner schools worldwide and funding for over 40,000 students and academics.
59   United States State Department, *Cultural Diplomacy – the Linchpin of Public Diplomacy: Report of the Advisory Committee on Cultural Diplomacy*, 2005: http://www.state.gov/documents/organization/54374.pdf (Retrieved August 2015).
60   Milton C. Cummings Jr., *Cultural Diplomacy and the United States Government: A Survey*, Washington, D.C., Center for Arts and Culture, 2003.
61   Kirsten Bound, Rachel Briggs, John Holden, Samuel Jones, *Cultural Diplomacy*, Demos, 2007: http://www.demos.co.uk/files/Cultural%20 diplomacy%20-%20web.pdf (Retrieved August 2015).

well-established cultural institutions such as the Alliance Française, the British Council or the Goethe Institute, are able to manage this tension constructively. The more recently established Confucius Institute is an interesting addition to this category, although its activities are more clearly identified with Chinese Government policy.

Sport is a significant component of cultural relations.[62] For instance, major sporting events are an opportunity for countries to burnish their brand image. Examples of such a phenomenon include the Olympic Games in Barcelona in 1992, in Beijing in 2008, and in London in 2012.

3.5 Public relations

Public relations, the art of getting people to think well of you, is arguably as old an activity as diplomacy itself and has become a fully-fledged profession as well as a multi-billion dollar business. Being applicable to all walks of life, it has not become a narrowly defined institution in the same way as diplomacy. Much like negotiation, public relations stretches more widely than diplomacy, while at the same time being only a part of what diplomacy is.

Modern public relations have been strongly influenced by the work of two acknowledged early 20th Century pioneers, Edward Louis Bernays and Ivy Ledbetter Lee. In 1906, responding to newspaper accusations of manipulation, Lee issued a "Declaration of Principles", which included the following passage:

> *".... our plan is, frankly and openly, on behalf of business and public institutions, to supply the press and public of the United States prompt and accurate information concerning subjects which it is of value and interest to the public to know about."* [63]

Writing in 1923, Bernays said:

> *"The three main elements of public relations are practically as old as society: informing people, persuading people, or integrating people with people. Of course, the means and methods of accomplishing these ends have changed as society has changed."* [64]

---

62   A famous instance of sport as diplomacy was the invitation to the United States table tennis team to visit China in 1971. This was one of a series of ice-breaking gestures that preceded President Nixon's visit to China in 1972, and which led to the establishment of diplomatic relations between China and the United States. This episode was inevitably characterised in the popular press as "ping pong diplomacy". See, for example, Public Broadcasting Service (PBS) American Experience: http://www.pbs.org/wgbh/amex/china/peopleevents/pande07.html (Retrieved August 2015).
For an interesting series of case studies of the use of sport in diplomacy, see Stuart Murray (ed), *Sports Diplomacy*, The Hague Journal of Diplomacy, 2013, Volume 8, Numbers 3-4.
63   For a critical account of the events surrounding Lee's declaration, and of the work of Edward Bernays (see below), *Public Relations – Rise of the Image Men*, The Economist, 16 December 2010: http://www.economist.com/node/17722733 (Retrieved August 2015).
64   Edward Bernays, *Crystallizing Public Opinion* (1923), Kindle Edition, Open Road Media, 2015.

The current definition of public relations by the Public Relations Society of America (PRSA) underlines the significance of strategic communication:

> *"Public relations is a strategic communication process that builds mutually beneficial relationships with organizations and their publics."* [65]

The Chartered Institute of Public Relations in the UK places emphasis on reputation management:

> *"Public relations is about reputation – the result of what you do, what you say and what others say about you."* [66]

This latter definition reminds us that a key aim of public relations, one that distinguishes it from advertising, is to get others to speak well of the organisation or individual concerned. If a company claims special qualities for its products, the consumer may or may not believe it. If one consumer tells another that the products in question possess these qualities, the claim becomes that much more credible.

This principle applies to public diplomacy generally[67], and to nation branding in particular: the good word spread by happy tourists or satisfied investors is worth far more than a paid advertising campaign. There is however a tendency for some governments, rather than simply abiding by this principle, to hire public relations companies at considerable expense to manufacture schemes to enhance their image. Public relations companies have undoubted expertise to bring to bear. Nevertheless, they cannot, however expensively, shift perceptions that are based on real experiences.

3.6 Lobbying

The essence of lobbying is that it is a very particular activity, highly targeted and personal. The activities of professional lobbyists on Capitol Hill in Washington are an example of lobbying in its most highly developed form. Nevertheless, lobbying is a universal phenomenon. A diplomat making a demarche to a foreign ministry, a non-governmental organisation seeking the release of a political prisoner, or children trying to persuade their parents to give them more pocket money – all are engaged in lobbying.

The principles of lobbying are the same as those for public diplomacy: knowing what you want, knowing your audience and being adequately prepared. The distinction lies in the narrower, specific focus of lobbying.

---

65   The Public Relations Society of America: http://prsa.org/pressroom/aboutpr.htm (Retrieved August 2015).
66   Chartered Institute of Public Relations (CIPR): http://www.cipr.co.uk/content/careers-cpd/careers-pr/what-pr (Retrieved August 2015).
67   An example of this principle in action can be seen in American efforts to persuade European publics of the virtue of deploying intermediate nuclear forces (INF) in the 1980s. The US Ambassador to NATO worked through regional opinion makers (journalists, members of think tanks, etc.) to get the American position across. See Nicholas J. Cull, *CPD Perspectives on Public Diplomacy: Public Diplomacy Lessons from the Past*, University of Southern California, Centre on Public Diplomacy at the Annenberg School, 2009; and Joseph S. Nye Jr., Soft Power: *The Means to Success in World Politics*, New York, Public Affairs, 2004.

Four different styles of lobbying have been identified, ranging from generating a common vision, through creating participation and trust, to applying rewards and pressure, and finally to logical persuasion. The first two of these fall into the "pull" mode of lobbying, and tend to be more effective when attempting to exert long-term influence on a target audiences with existing strong views or vested interests, especially when the lobbyer has no recognised power base and the relationship is new, or has a history of mistrust.

The latter two are in the "push" mode of lobbying and work best when the target audience is relatively ignorant or has no threatened vested interest, and recognises the legitimacy of the lobbyer's power. All these styles, or a blend thereof, may be appropriate according to circumstances. But for developing committed attitude change, the most effective mix is "pull", combined with the minimum amount of "push" to achieve compliance.[68]

Lobbying is best done face-to-face and may occur in an informal setting, such as over a drink or a meal, or in an arranged meeting. The latter has the advantage of being more honest and straightforward, but may not allow for the more subtle and relaxed interaction of an informal meeting. Use of the telephone (including texting) may be necessary, because of urgency or physical distance, but is less satisfactory in the near-absence of personal interaction. E-mail and use of social networks is even less satisfactory, because such interaction as there is, however rapid, will not be contemporaneous. However, it may be desirable, or even unavoidable, if there is a complex and detailed case to be made, or if the target audience is numerous and geographically widespread. Depending on the circumstances, a blend of the aforementioned approaches may prove to be the most effective.

3.7 Conclusions

All the activities examined above have a relationship to public diplomacy. In some cases (nation branding, propaganda, cultural relations), they overlap with public diplomacy – and some commentators would argue that they are integral to public diplomacy. In others (public relations, lobbying), the principles and techniques are relevant to public diplomacy, while the activities themselves are much wider in scope.

Much of the debate about all these activities is semantic: one man's propaganda can be defined as another man's public diplomacy. Irrespective of the specific techniques involved, the essential principles common to them all are: know your message and know your audience.

---

68   These styles are analysed in detail in an e-learning package, *Strategic Thinking*, prepared for the British Foreign and Commonwealth Office in 2008 by Walkgrove Limited.

Chapter 4

Historical Development of Public Diplomacy

4.1 Introduction

Having looked at definitions of public diplomacy, and of related activities, in this chapter we shall consider public diplomacy from a historical perspective. Much of the recent material derives, inevitably, from American experience, since the United States has been in the forefront of public diplomacy developments. However, as we shall see, the origins of public diplomacy long pre-date the existence of the United States.

4.2 Before the Cold War

"There is nothing new under the sun." [69]

Public Diplomacy did not spring fully formed into existence with the coining of the expression in 1965. Diplomacy itself is often described as the second oldest profession[70], so it is reasonable to look a long way back into history for evidence of activity similar to what we today enshrine in the term public diplomacy. Jan Melissen, for example, has observed that:

"It is tempting to see public diplomacy as old wine in new bottles." [71]

The cases Melissen offers over the centuries to illustrate this observation are persuasive: Greek orators addressing the assembled worthies in fellow city states; medieval princes making extravagant shows of wealth when visiting their counterparts; the use of printing by Cardinal Richelieu and others to distribute political pamphlets to a wide audience around Europe; and the massive expression of state power (i.e. of nation branding) that was Louis XIV's Palace of Versailles. Closer to our times, Melissen describes the re-branding of Turkey as a modern, secular state under Kemal Attaturk and the use of propaganda (see Chapter 3) by the Nazis and their opponents. One way or another, governments have been seeking to influence their own populations, and others', since time immemorial.

What characterises changes in diplomacy in the last two hundred years – and more – is that they have been in response to major technological, economic and societal change. In the 19th Century, the advent of the telegraph, and of steam and rail travel, accelerated and multiplied the movement of both people and information. The growth of the press and the movement away from absolute monarchies to constitutional monarchies or republics made it increasingly difficult for governments to ignore the views of wider publics, either their own or those in other countries. Further technological advances in the 20th Century (such as air travel, the cinema, radio and television) brought new threats and opportunities[72] to governments in their desire to shape public opinion.

---

69   Ecclesiastes 1.9, *The Bible*, English Standard Version 2001.

70   Although some would grant this accolade to espionage. See, e.g., Philip Knightly, *The Second Oldest Profession: Spies and Spying in the Twentieth Century*, London, Andre Deutsch, 1986.

71   Jan Melissen (ed), 2005.

72   The Nazis were very quick to use the cinema as a propaganda instrument. On the allied side, the period leading up the Second World War saw the birth of two institutions in the United Kingdom that were to prove enduring: the BBC World Service and the British Council.

The United States was involved early in its existence in public diplomacy. At the end of the 18th Century, Benjamin Franklin and Thomas Jefferson used their access to elite groups and to the media in London and Paris to put the case for the American colonies to both the British and French people. The United States was also a pioneer in creating relevant institutions: President Wilson formed the Committee on Public Information in 1917 (although it did not survive the end of the First World War) and President Roosevelt established the Office of War Information and The Voice of America during the Second World War.[73] Before its entry into the war, the United States itself was on the receiving end of a successful British public diplomacy campaign to persuade Americans to support the struggle against the Nazis.[74]

4.3 During the Cold War

By the end of the Second World War governments were engaged in a range of activities readily recognisable today as part of the public diplomacy toolkit: speech-making; sponsored visits; cultural and educational exchange; exhibitions; seminars and conferences; outward and inward missions; broadcasting; and media management.

The ideological struggle between liberalism and communism, which had first manifested itself at the end of the First World War, had been temporarily in abeyance during the war against fascism. With the defeat of the Axis powers, after a brief interlude of relative tranquillity, this struggle re-emerged as the defining characteristic of the post-war period: the Cold War. It was inevitably dominated by the two countries that were then the only super powers: the United States and the Soviet Union.

Both sides in the Cold War saw the struggle in existential terms. The focus was on military and economic supremacy, with the threat of mutual nuclear extinction the main constraint on war between the parties – although there was conflict by proxy in various theatres, such as in Korea and Vietnam. As an adjunct to the military stand-off, each side invested substantial effort in attempts to win the battle of minds, both in each other's countries and in third countries – a process encouraged by the emergence of new nations during the decolonisation of the 1960s and 1970s. The intensity of this psychological warfare, and whether the emphasis was on tarnishing the image and credibility of one's opponent or advocating one's own virtues, varied throughout the period according to each side's perception of their relative strength and of the prospects for peaceful accommodation.

In the United States, the Cold War stimulated the establishment of the United States Information Agency (USIA), as well as of Radio Free Europe and Radio Liberty, key institutions in the psychological battle that contributed towards the eventual demise of communism. For all the success of the United States' public diplomacy during the Cold War, it was arguably inhibited by a number of factors. First, there was the unresolved debate, reflected in the attitude of different administrations, between those who advocated public diplomacy as a strategic tool of foreign and national security policy and those who perceived it as

73   US Diplomacy – An Online Exploration of Diplomatic History and Foreign Affairs: http://www.usdiplomacy.org/diplomacytoday/contemporary/public.php (Retrieved August 2015).
74   Nicholas J. Cull, *Public Diplomacy – CPD Perspectives on Public Diplomacy: Lessons from the Past*, University of Southern California Centre on Public Diplomacy at the Annenberg School, 2009.

an objective information operation. Secondly, there was confusion as to whether elites or masses should constitute target audiences. Finally, there was the question as to whether the USIA should be involved in policy-making, to which the answer for the most part seems to have been negative.[75, 76]

Other countries were active during the period in re-building their national images (for example, Germany and Japan after the war; Spain after the death of Franco; and Britain, France and others after shedding their colonial territories). Largely absent from the public diplomacy scene, for the most part, were the newly independent countries of the developing world.

4.4 After the Cold War

The collapse of the Soviet Union, and the emergence of the United States as the sole superpower, was seen in the West as heralding a new dawn, the final triumph of liberal democracy.[77]

Along with the peace dividend to be earned from the reduction in military expenditure permitted by the end of the Cold War, came the belief by both the United States and its allies that the need to expend resources on public diplomacy was also reduced. Budgets were cut, and the USIA was folded into the State Department.[78]

Public diplomacy did not grind to a halt during this period. But in the absence of a major ideological foe, the promotional activities of many western countries were principally focused on material issues such as trade, investment and tourism.

At the same time, the interlinked phenomena of globalisation and the end of the Cold War brought with them new challenges and new conflicts. These are examined in more detail below and in Chapter 5.

4.5 After 9/11

The trauma of 9/11 and other atrocities committed by Al-Qaeda revealed the vulnerability of countries to the asymmetric threat of terrorism, causing governments to increase their efforts, both individually and collectively to develop counter-strategies. While the focus was on intelligence and interdiction, the role of public diplomacy in building bridges between cultures was also recognized as important in light of the troubled relationship between the West and the Islamic World.

75   Carnes Lord and Hella Dale, *Public Diplomacy and the Cold War: Lessons learned*, The Heritage Foundation, Number 2070, 18 September 2007: http://www.heritage.org/research/reports/2007/09/public-diplomacy-and-the-cold-war-lessons-learned (Retrieved August 2015).
76   Edward R. Murrow, when accepting President Kennedy's invitation to be become head of the USIA is famously reported to have said: "If you want me to be there on the crash-landings, I better be there on the takeoff." (See, e.g., Richard Halloran, 2007.) But Murrow seems to have been exceptional in this regard.
77   See, in particular, Francis Fukuyama, *The End of History and the Last Man*, London, Penguin, 1992.
78   Kenneth H. Nakamura and Matthew C. Weed, *US Public Diplomacy: Background and Current Issues*, Congressional Research Service, 18 December 2009.

Early American efforts in the "shared values campaign" were seen by many in the targeted countries as naive propaganda, and claimed by critics to be inconsistent with United States military action in Afghanistan and Iraq. In 2007, the Bush administration published the United States National Strategy for Public Diplomacy and Strategic Communication, the first plan of its kind designed to be implemented in all government agencies. The three strategic objectives identified in the plan were to offer people across the world a vision of hope based on American values, to marginalise violent extremists, and to nurture and foster common interests.

New initiatives taken by the United States included the establishment of the Digital Outreach Team, who use interactive media to try to correct misinformation about the United States.[79] On assuming office, President Obama made communicating with the world a personal priority and sought to address concerns about interagency coordination – not least because of the increased public diplomacy activity of the Department of Defense – with emphasis on the need to synchronise deeds with words.[80]

9/11 also triggered a debate on public diplomacy in the wider world, making it an issue for most foreign ministries. The motivation for governments engaging in public diplomacy was diverse. Candidate countries for membership of the European Union invested in programmes to persuade sceptical European publics that they would be worthy members. Developing countries aimed at securing economic assistance. In some cases, public diplomacy activity was inspired by a specific event (such as the Bali bombing, which stimulated a campaign by Indonesia to enhance its image). Rising economic powers such as China and India embraced ambitions for self-projection on the world stage. Jan Melissen contends, however, that the strongest growth in public diplomacy is to be discerned in highly interdependent regions and between countries linked by multiple transactional relationships, with a high degree of connectedness between civil societies. Examples are the relationships between the member countries of the European Union and between the United States and Canada.[81]

4.6 The public diplomacy of international organisations

Since the Second World War, there has been extraordinary growth in institutionalised multilateralism. At both global and regional level, a host of international organisations have been formed in the attempt by states to grapple collaboratively with the complex and sometimes apparently intractable problems they face.

Most international organisations have significant press and information operations. Usually, although not exclusively, these are aimed at educating the publics in their member states and are therefore akin to the "domestic socialisation" practised by states in a bid to bring their publics along with their policies (although, as we shall see in Chapter 5, the distinction between this and public diplomacy is no longer as straightforward as it used to be).

---

79   *Ibid.*
80   See, for example, the National Framework for Strategic Communication, submitted to Congress in 2010 and updated in 2012. In 2010, the State Department also released its Strategic Framework for Public Diplomacy.
81   Jan Melissen (ed), 2005.

The United Nations, for example, has an extensive public information operation, employing all the public diplomacy tools and techniques we shall be examining in Part 2 of this book. The UN Department of Public Information runs a worldwide network of UN Information Centres (UNICs), which translate information material into local languages, engage opinion-makers, place op-ed articles by senior UN officials in the national media, and organize events to highlight particular issues.[82]

The European Union is an example of an international organisation whose public diplomacy stretches beyond its membership – even though much of it is, in fact, aimed at publics in member states, and categorised as extravagant propaganda by euro-sceptic critics.[83] The EU's communication strategy for enlargement is designed to explain the goals and responsibilities of the European project to countries aspiring to membership; the European Neighbourhood Policy is directed towards the EU's immediate neighbours that have not been offered the prospect of membership; and, through its worldwide network of overseas delegations, the EU seeks to assert itself on the international stage. The EU's considerable soft power, deriving in part from its economic and political success – though somewhat diminished by the recent crisis in the euro zone – has been extremely effective in its near neighbourhood. Public diplomacy efforts in the wider world have, however, been less successful.[84,85] Hopes that the creation of the External Action Service in 2010 would facilitate greater coherence have yet to be fully realised, although much progress has been made.[86]

An organisation that has seen significant change in the last decade in its public diplomacy activity is the North Atlantic Treaty Organisation (NATO). In line with its internal reforms and increased military engagement, most notably in Afghanistan, NATO has moved from a simple information operation to seeking to develop a series of dedicated communication strategies – requiring harmonisation of the military and civilian approaches to communication – designed to explain its role both to publics in member countries and to the wider world.[87]

The overwhelming difficulty for most international organisations in practising public diplomacy resides in their intrinsic nature: they are not sovereign states and cannot take major initiatives without the acquiescence – and funding – of their member states, who themselves have to achieve consensus on the issues concerned. In the case of the EU, where some competences have been surrendered by the member states (but others, notably in the field of foreign and security policy, have not), this can cause significant institutional tension.

82   See the UNIC website: http://unic.un.org/aroundworld/unics/en/whoWeAre/aboutDPI/index.asp (Retrieved August 2015).
83   See, for example, Lee Rotherham and Lorraine Mullaly, *The hard sell: EU communication policy and the campaign for hearts and mind*, Open Europe, December 2008: http://archive.openeurope.org.uk/Content/documents/Pdfs/hardsell.pdf (Retrieved August 2015)
84   See, the EU website: http://europa.eu/index_en.htm (Retrieved August 2015).
85   A paper produced for the London-based Foreign Policy Centre in 2005 argued that the way the EU communicated with third-country publics was atomized and disjointed and that the capacity of the EU institutions to engage in public diplomacy activities was limited by lack of resources and political will. See Philip Fiske de Gouveia and Hester Plumridge, *European Infopolitik: Developing EU Public Diplomacy Strategy*, The Foreign Policy Centre, 2005: http://fpc.org.uk/fsblob/657.pdf (Retrieved August 2015).
86   One recent study has suggested that the creation of the EEAS has further complicated the EU's institutional arrangements, making coherent communication even more difficult than hitherto. See Vicky Reynaart, *The European Union's Foreign Policy since the Treaty of Lisbon: The Difficult Quest for More Consistency and Coherence*, The Hague Journal of Diplomacy, 2012, Volume 7, Number 2.
87   For an assessment of the challenges NATO has encountered in this regard, see Stephanie Babst, *Reinventing NATO's Public Diplomacy*, Research Paper, NATO Defense College, November 2008, Number 41. See also the NATO website: http://www.nato.int/cps/en/natolive/index.htm (Retrieved August 2015).

4.7 Conclusions

The 21st Century environment to which public diplomacy (and diplomacy in general) has to adapt is complex and ever-changing. The ICT revolution means that governments have lost their near monopoly over control of information: through the Internet, 24-hour television and mobile telephony, information is now available instantly to vast numbers of people around the globe. The ubiquity of the media renders it near impossible to make and execute policy in total secrecy. The growth of democracy in ever more countries, and changes in society, mean that governments are increasingly answerable to their people. The blurring of the distinction between domestic and overseas policies has created an equivalent blurring between public diplomacy and "domestic socialisation". There are also increasing numbers of non-state actors, ranging from the most benign of non-governmental organisations (NGOs) to terrorist groups like Al-Qaeda, disseminating their messages cost-effectively through readily accessible international networks. Such phenomena have rendered old models of public diplomacy, involving the one-way transmission of information, increasingly problematic. These issues (and how governments respond to them) are examined further in Chapter 5.

Public Diplomacy: What it is - and how to do it

Chapter 5

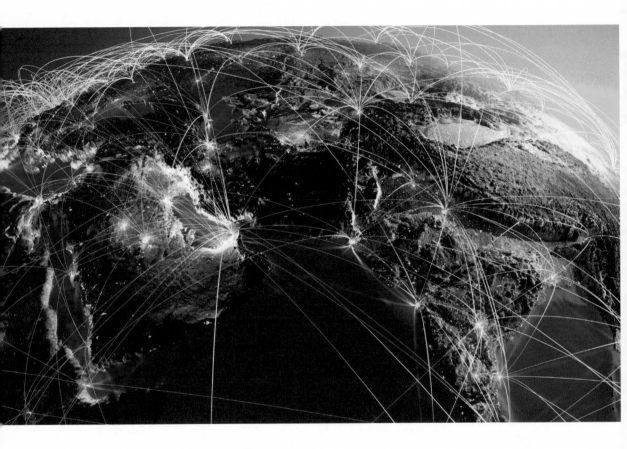

The Changing Global Environment

Flight connections in the Middle East and Asia
Shutterstock_110973785

5.1 Introduction

Public diplomacy – or something very similar, even if not so described – has been practised for many centuries. The environment in which diplomacy is practised has however changed over the years and is now changing ever more rapidly. In this chapter we shall look at different aspects of this change: the ICT revolution, the 24-hour media, the growth in democracy, the blurring of the distinction between domestic and overseas issues, the increasing significance of non-state actors, and the rise of citizen diplomacy.

5.2 The ICT revolution

Human communication has experienced dramatic change throughout history. Most fundamental of all was the advent of language itself, a development about which we can only speculate, despite all that has been written on the subject. The development of written language, permitting the creation of permanent records, was another giant leap forward. All subsequent change has arguably been marginal when compared to these monumental shifts in our ability to exchange information and ideas.[88]

Yet there have been further momentous developments. The invention of the printing press in the 15th Century permitted the dissemination of pamphlets to a wide audience. Travel by steamship and rail in the 19th Century, and by air in the 20th, allowed people with means to visit hitherto remote lands with relative ease. The invention of the telegraph in the 19th Century truly revolutionised communication, allowing for the first time information exchange over long distances in something close to real time. This was arguably the beginning of the information and communications technology revolution we are currently experiencing.

As a result of technological change, governments have been steadily losing their near monopoly on information. What characterises the current environment is the pace of that change. Developments in the Internet and mobile telephony in the last decade alone mean that information about events can be available instantly to vast numbers of people around the world, frequently even before governments themselves are aware of these events.

Some illustrative statistics make the point. The Facebook website recorded 1.49 billion monthly active members as at 30 June 2015 (compared with 67 million in 2007). 1.31 billion of these accessed Facebook via mobile devices. There are 316 million monthly active Twitter members (80% via mobile devices), who altogether send 500 million tweets a day.[89]

Where America goes, the world frequently follows. According to a 2013 survey by the Annenberg Institute at the University of Southern California, 86% of the population of the United States in 2012 over the age of seventeen regularly went on line (for those of this group under the age of twenty-four, the figure was close to 100%). Of people using the Internet, 79% used Twitter, Facebook or another form of social media, while 97% used e-mail. 79% regarded the Internet as an important or very important information source (compared with 55% for newspapers and 66% for television). 50% had trust/lots of trust in the Internet information, while 9% had trust in only a small proportion. The 2014 survey reveals

88   See, for example, Maggie Tallerman and Kathleen R Gibson (ed), *The Oxford Handbook of Language Evolution*, Oxford University Press, 2011.
89   http://newsroom.fb.com/company-info/ (Retrieved August 2015); https://about.twitter.com/company (Retrieved August 2015).

that in 2013 Americans spent an average of 21 hours a week online, and 68% did so via mobile devices.[90]

The developing world is rapidly catching up in Internet use. This is shown by the following estimates from the ITU/World Telecommunications/ICT Indicators Database[91] of Internet use in 2013 compared with four years earlier:

	2013	(2009)
World Population:	7.1b	(6.8b)
Using Internet:	2.6b	(1.1b)
Developed countries	1.3b	(0.7b)
Developing countries	1.3b	(0.4b)
Fixed	0.7b	(0.5b)
Mobile	1.9b	(0.6b)

The implications of these technological changes are clear. It is not simply that information can be disseminated globally in real time. The rapid growth in trans-boundary networks permits transmission and exchange of opinion and wide scale lobbying, acculturation and calls to action by a range of non-state actors (see below). The Arab Spring of 2011 provides a graphic example of the contribution of social networks towards energising and mobilising social change.

In Part 2 of this book, we shall consider how governments are responding to the challenge posed by new media in the public diplomacy field.

5.3 The 24-hour media

The ubiquity of the traditional media – the so-called CNN factor – is a less recent phenomenon than the surge in new media. Governments have for some time had to adjust to the virtual impossibility of generating and implementing policies in total secrecy.[92] Working in the glare of publicity is a constant challenge, and real-time media management is essential to success. We shall be examining the relevant techniques in Part 2.

5.4 Growth in democracy

We have seen how the move towards constitutional monarchies and republics in the 19th Century, coupled with the rise of the press, made governments increasingly aware of the need to cultivate public opinion. Until the middle of the 20th Century, however, many of the world's peoples were subjects of colonial powers and had no national voice of their own. Following the Second World War came a wave

---

90   2013 USC Annenberg Digital Future Report:
http://www.digitalcenter.org/wp-content/uploads/2013/06/2013-Report.pdf (Retrieved August 2015).
The 2014 Digital Future Report, USC Annenberg School Center for the Digital – Future:
http://www.digitalcenter.org/wp-content/uploads/2014/12/2014-Digital-Future-Report.pdf (Retrieved August 2015).
91   Estimate from ITU/World Telecommunication/ICT Indicators Database: http://www.itu.int/pub/D-IND-WTID.OL (Retrieved August 2015).
92   Graham Allison and Philip Zelikow have drawn attention to the fact that the Kennedy Administration, when handling the Cuban missile crisis in 1962, had several days in which secretly to debate policy before the true nature of the threat came into the public domain. Such a luxury would be unthinkable today. See Graham Allison and Philip Zelikow, *Essence of Decision*, 2nd edition, Boston, Addison Wesley Longman, 1999.

of decolonisation, producing new independent nations, a process repeated later with the break-up of the Soviet Union. In the wake of this expansion of the numbers of independent countries came a drive towards greater democratisation, a drive that gained impetus from the technological change discussed above.

According to Freedom House, there were 122 electoral democracies in 2013, 63% of a total of 195 independent countries. By comparison, there were only 69 electoral democracies in 1989, 41% of a total of 167 countries.

In a historical listing of countries categorised as free, partly free or not free, the figures were as follows:

Year	Total	Free	Partly Free	Not Free
2013	195 (100%)	88 (45%)	59 (30%)	48 (25%)
1989	167 (100%)	61 (37%)	44 (26%)	62 (37%)
1972	151 (100%)	44 (29%)	38 (25%)	69 (46%)

Freedom House: Freedom in the World, 2014

There has in fact been a slight decline since 2006, both in the numbers of electoral democracies (down from 123) and of free countries (down from 90).[93, 94] Nevertheless, the general trend over the last forty years is clear: the number of independent countries has increased significantly, as has the proportion of them enjoying a greater or lesser degree of democracy.

This process of rapid democratisation, however incomplete, means that governments are increasingly more accountable, and in thrall to public opinion when developing policy. And if governments care more and more about what their publics think, then other governments care too – and aim to try to influence that thinking.

5.5 The blurring of the distinction between domestic and international issues

In the 21st Century the nations of the world confront a series of problems susceptible to solution only by collaborative effort. Climate change, health threats such as AIDS and influenza pandemics, international crime, terrorism, human rights abuses and economic crises, all these and more require governments to work together towards common solutions.

93   Freedom House, Freedom in the World, 2014: http://www.freedomhouse.org/report/freedom-world/freedom-world-2014 (Retrieved August 2015).
94   The Economist Intelligence Unit (EIU) Democracy Index, employing slightly different categories, tells a similar story, including a slight decline in recent years. In 2013, of 167 countries surveyed, 25 were classed as full democracies, 54 as flawed democracies, 36 as hybrid and 52 authoritarian. The EIU Democracy Index 2013: http://www.eiu.com/public/thankyou_download.aspx?activity=download&campaignid=Democracy0814 (Retrieved August 2015).

Many of the issues under discussion have traditionally been regarded as matters of domestic policy, but this distinction is becoming ever more difficult to sustain. Environmental pollution does not respect international borders, nor do financial crises. Ease of air travel assists the spread of disease and, together with the ICT revolution, facilitates international crime and terrorism. The international media and social networks remind us constantly of human rights abuses.

The inability to separate the foreign from the domestic has impelled governments into new ways of organising themselves, so that domestic expertise (both governmental and otherwise) is properly integrated into overseas policies, and that domestic policies are in harmony. In the public diplomacy field this inability to separate internal and external policies has also served to blur the distinction between public diplomacy, i.e. seeking to influence publics overseas, and domestic socialisation, i.e. bringing one's own public along with government policy. Governments certainly seek to maintain the distinction, but in practice, given international media coverage and the Internet, it is virtually impossible to impart a different message to a domestic audience from the one being given to audiences overseas.

5.6 The increasing significance of non-state actors

International relations have historically been conducted between states. This remains the case. But the international stage is becoming ever more crowded with non-state actors, whose actions can contribute towards the success or failure of states' attempts to resolve the issues they confront.

The first of these non-state actors are the multinational corporations some of whom have assets and income in excess of those of many nation states. The economic power of MNCs is considerable, and governments need to strike a balance in order to regulate their behaviour to ensure probity without stifling economic activity. MNCs also deploy formidable public relations resources.

As powerful in their different ways, are non-governmental organisations. These are so varied in size and resources as to make generalisations about them difficult. Some, such as Greenpeace, Oxfam and Amnesty International, dispose of considerable resources and expertise and are extremely influential. But even NGOs with slender resources can exert considerable influence by judicious use of the Internet and social networks.

A particular kind of NGO is a terrorist network like Al Qaeda. Such networks have learned to use the Internet to devastating effect, frequently getting their message across more effectively than the governments seeking to defeat them.[95]

Governments cannot ignore the activities of these organisations. They must work with them if their intentions are benign and combat them when not (see, for example, the United States "Digital Outreach" team, established in 2006). Not engaging at all runs the risk of ceding the argument.[96]

---

95   Witness the view of the Singaporean diplomat, Kishore Mahbubani, when asked in 2005 what puzzled him about America's battle with Osama bin Laden: "How has one man in a cave managed to out-communicate the world's greatest communication society?" Quoted in Richard Halloran, 2007.

96   For example, when the International Fund for Animal Welfare (IFAW) created an online "meeting space" in Second Life about seal hunting, the Canadian Government did not participate and found itself at a disadvantage in world public opinion. See http://www.ifaw.org/us/node/1504 (Retrieved August 2015).

5.7 Citizen diplomacy

Citizen diplomacy has been defined by the United States Centre for Citizen Diplomacy (USCCD) as:

> *"… the engagement of individual citizens in programs and activities primarily in the voluntary, private sector that increase cross-cultural understanding and knowledge between people from different cultures and countries, leading to a greater mutual respect."* [97]

Citizen diplomacy is highly developed in the United States. There are an estimated 8,000 non-governmental based organisations providing opportunities for volunteers and others to be involved in international programmes in, inter alia, sport, schools, universities, youth organisations, performing and visual arts, the environment and global health. American organisations have not historically worked in coalition with similar organisations from other countries. However, the USCCD has recently joined with the British Council and others to explore the potential of forming an International Alliance for Global Citizenship.[98]

When citizen diplomacy is focused on efforts to pursue solutions to disputes that governments have been unable to resolve, it assumes the mantle of track II diplomacy. A significant example of the latter are the unofficial discussions between Israeli and Arab scholars, journalists and former government and military officials which have been taking place since soon after the 1967 Six Day War and have often paved the way for subsequent official negotiations (talks in 1992 and 1993, for example, led to the Oslo Accords).[99]

Citizen diplomacy throws up a similar conundrum to that we have observed in the case of cultural relations (see Lesson 3). Its value in enhancing the cross-cultural understanding desired by governments derives from the autonomy, and thus credibility, of the individual citizens involved. However, this autonomy may lead to actions which themselves are inconsistent with government policy.[100]

5.8 Responses of governments to the changing environment

How are governments responding to the challenges of this rapidly changing environment? It is a very mixed picture.

The fundamental difficulty for governments (and perhaps, above all for foreign ministries), is that they are operating in a hierarchical, vertical tradition in a world that is becoming progressively more networked and horizontal.[101] Governments' responses to this difficulty are diverse and inevitably reflect the nature of their societies and political systems.

---

97   Ann Olsen Schodde, President and CEO of USCCD, *Building a Nation of Global Citizen Diplomats*, Public Diplomacy magazine, 20 April 2012: http://publicdiplomacymagazine.com/citizen-diplomacy-building-a-nation-of-global-citizen-diplomats/ (Retrieved August 2015).
98   *Ibid.*
99   For an authoritative account of Track II talks on the Middle East, see: Hussein Agha, Shai Feldman, Ahmad Khalidi and Zeev Schiff, *Track-II Diplomacy: Lessons from the Middle East*, Cambridge, The MIT Press, 2004.
100   This point is well argued in an article by Joseph S. Nye Jr., *The Pros and Cons of Citizen Diplomacy*, published in the International Herald Tribune, 4 October 2010.
101   For a more detailed exposition of these models, see Brian Hocking in Jan Melissen (ed), 2005.

Some have not moved away from the old, hierarchical model, with their public diplomacy, such as it is, very much an "add-on" to conventional diplomacy. They have for the most part embraced the new technologies, but their mode is still very much that of one-way messaging. This need not preclude a degree of success. China, for example, has developed an integrated public diplomacy, the aim of which is to reassure the world of China's "peaceful rise". It is easier in an authoritarian system to get everyone speaking with the same voice. However, the downside is the difficulty of adapting in good time to the networked world, when there is weak civil society and no tradition of independent thought.[102]

Others, in particular (and understandably) countries that have relatively recently obtained their independence, or feel a need to redress long-standing negative perceptions, are still in the nation branding mode.[103]

Yet others have sought to do new things. For example:

i. The Canadian government led collaboration spanning domestic and international actors, both public and private (the "Ottawa process") in the campaign to have landmines banned.[104]

ii. In 2007 Sweden opened a "virtual" Embassy on Second Life.[105] It was not a resounding success, and was closed at the end of 2012.

iii. The United States is active in employing the Internet in a variety of ways, with varying success, under the general rubric of Public Diplomacy 2.0.[106] In 2011, for example, a virtual embassy was launched to allow Iranian citizens access to information about the United States.

iv. Most foreign ministry websites now employ blogs, Facebook, Twitter, YouTube, Flickr and others to create a degree of interactivity on their websites.[107]

Overall the record is uneven, and the essential challenge for governments remains. There are many voices in the blogosphere, of which theirs is only one. To have any hope of being heard, governments must have a coherent, coordinated strategy and be prepared to engage constructively with these other voices. It is easy to say this. It is not easy to achieve.

---

102   Jan Melissen (ed), 2005.
103   The Council on Foreign Relations describes how Slovenia and Croatia launched major campaigns following the break-up of Yugoslavia to distinguish themselves clearly from Belgrade: http://www.cfr.org/information-and-communication/nation-branding-explained/p14776#p6 (Retrieved August 2015).
For an account of attempts at nation-branding by post-Soviet States, see Erica Marrat, *Nation Branding in Central Asia: A New Campaign to Present Ideas about the State and the Nation*, Europe-Asia Studies, September 2009, Volume 61, Number 7, pp. 1123–1136: http://www.tandfonline.com/doi/abs/10.1080/09668130903068657?journalCode=ceas20 (retrieved August 2015).
Colombia's campaign to shift its image away from drugs and violence is described in *"Colombia is Passion": Has nation branding worked for Colombia?*, Public and Cultural Diplomacy module at London Metropolitan University, 27 March 2011: http://publicandculturaldiplomacyd.blogspot.co.uk/2011/03/colombia-is-passionhas-nation-branding.html (Retrieved August 2015).
104   The Ottawa Process is frequently cited as an example of collaboration between governments and NGOs to achieve a valuable goal that would have been difficult to achieve without such cooperation. For a more critical appraisal, raising questions about the significance of the involvement of NGOs, see Nicola Short, *The Role of NGOs in the Ottawa Process to Ban Landmines*, International Negotiation, Kluwer Law International, 1999, Volume 4, pp. 481–500: http://faculty.maxwell.syr.edu/rdenever/IntlSecurity2008_docs/Short_NGOsOttawa.pdf (Retrieved August 2015).
105   See: https://secondhouseofsweden.wordpress.com/ (Retrieved August 2015).
106   For an interesting case study, see Lina Khatib, William Dutton and Michael Thelwall, *Public Diplomacy 2.0: An Exploratory Case Study of the US Digital Outreach Team*, CDDRL Working Papers, 2011, Number 120: http://cddrl.stanford.edu/publications/public_diplomacy_20_an_exploratory_case_study_of_the_digital_outreach_team (Retrieved August 2015). The authors conclude that technological advances will not automatically realize the vision of public diplomacy 2.0 without creative, strategic thinking about how to implement and use Web 2.0 most effectively in conversations among distrusting adversaries that are often hostile and suspicious. They also argue that, irrespective of how much the United States invests in developing public diplomacy methods, the best way to change attitudes and gain trust in the Middle East is through foreign policy that links words and deeds.
107   See, for example, the British Foreign and Commonwealth website: www.fco.gov.uk (Retrieved August 2015).

Chapter 6

The Legal Framework for Public Diplomacy

6.1 Introduction

We have so far considered definitions of public diplomacy (and of related activities), the impact of the concept of soft power, the historical development of public diplomacy and the changing environment in which it is practised.

What, however, is the legal framework within which public diplomacy is practised?

6.2 The Vienna Convention on Diplomatic Relations

Diplomatic practice has developed over the years largely through custom and precedent. Certain practices and entitlements, such as diplomatic immunity and the rules of precedence for ambassadors, have at different times been enshrined in treaties.[108] It was not, however, until the negotiation of the 1961 Vienna Convention on Diplomatic Relations that a comprehensive attempt was made to codify diplomatic activity. The Convention is the legal foundation on which bilateral diplomacy currently rests.[109]

The Vienna Convention says nothing about public diplomacy – the expression had in 1961 not yet entered into common diplomatic parlance. Nor does it explicitly refer to activities that would today be described as public diplomacy. The relevant article for our purpose, Article 3, dealing with the functions of diplomatic missions, reads as follows:

> 1. *"The functions of a diplomatic mission consist, inter alia, in*
>
> > *i. Representing the sending State in the receiving State;*
> > *II. Protecting in the receiving State the interests of the sending State and of its nationals, within the limits permitted by international law;*
> > *III. Negotiating with the Government of the receiving State;*
> > *IV. Ascertaining by all lawful means conditions and developments in the receiving State, and reporting thereon to the Government of the sending State;*
> > *V. Promoting friendly relations between the sending State and the receiving State, and developing their economic, cultural and scientific relations.*
>
> 2. *Nothing in the present Convention shall be construed as preventing the performance of consular functions by a diplomatic mission."* [110]

The list of functions in Article 3 is not exclusive (note the words "inter alia" in the opening sentence) and the functions listed have by and large been interpreted generously. Under the general umbrella of

108   For example, the Congress of Vienna in 1815 finally settled the prickly question of how seniority among ambassadors in a capital city should be determined. See Sir Ivor Roberts (ed), *Satow's Diplomatic Practice*, 6th edition, Oxford University Press, 2009.
109   Sir Ivor Roberts, 2009.
110   Vienna Convention on Diplomatic Relations, Vienna, 18 April 1961.

developing "economic relations", for example, embassies – or related organisations – undertake active promotion of trade, investment and tourism. As a matter of course, embassies also have sections devoted to dealing with the media and the public, which in the terms of the Convention might be interpreted as both representation and promoting friendly relations.

There is, however, one possible constraint on public diplomacy activity in the Vienna Convention, namely Article 41, the first clause of which reads as follows:

> "1. Without prejudice to their privileges and immunities, it is the duty of all persons enjoying such privileges and immunities to respect the laws and regulations of the receiving State. They also have a duty not to interfere in the internal affairs of that State." [111]

The acceptability, or otherwise, of specific public diplomacy activity appears therefore to rest on the interpretation of the receiving State as to what constitutes legality or interference in its internal affairs (see discussion of state sovereignty below).

6.3 Issues of state sovereignty

Chapter 1, Article 2.1 of the United Nations Charter (which takes precedence over all other international law) reads as follows:

> "1. The Organization is based on the principle of the sovereign equality of all its Members."

Article 2.7 reads:

> "7. Nothing contained in the present Charter shall authorize the United Nations to intervene in matters which are essentially within the domestic jurisdiction of any state...." [112]

The principle of state sovereignty (i.e. the Westphalian principle underpinning the society of states), which is enshrined in Article 2 of the United Nations Charter, does not prejudice the application of enforcement measures under Chapter VII of the Charter (i.e. when the United Nations Security Council has determined the existence of a threat to the peace, breach of the peace or act of aggression). Such cases are, however, by their nature, exceptional.

Taken in conjunction with the assertion of the Vienna Convention that states have a duty not to interfere in the internal affairs of other states, it would be reasonable to assume that there was a strong presumption on the part of states against public diplomacy activity designed to persuade publics to exert pressure on their governments in order to change their policies.

In fact, most governments today accept, indeed embrace, the concept of public diplomacy, at least in their public pronouncements. How far this avowed acceptance is translated into practical tolerance of specific public diplomacy activity varies considerably. Authoritarian governments, while themselves deploying public diplomacy techniques to manage their international image, look askance at the

111   *Ibid.*
112   Charter of the United Nations, signed on 26 June 1945 in San Francisco, entered into force on 24 October 1945.

unleashing of public opinion on such issues as democracy, human rights and the rule of law, which is seen as a threat to their ability to control this image – and indeed to internal stability. There is therefore little scope for engagement with civil societies in such states, who draw a clear line between what they regard as acceptable activity and interference in their internal affairs.[113, 114]

This line is not so easy to draw in democratic countries, even (or perhaps especially) in countries enjoying friendly relations, such as the member states of the EU. When ambassadors are encouraged by their governments to engage in public debate, it is not always clear when their actions spill over into domestic interference.[115]

6.4 Public diplomacy and public international law more generally

Public international law in general is reticent about public diplomacy, and the academic literature on public diplomacy is equally reticent about public international law. There have been attempts to remedy this absence of linkage, but these have tended to examine the deployment of international law in support of specific public diplomacy aims – and the damage to these aims when the law is flouted – or the contribution of public diplomacy campaigns to the creation of international law, such as the treaty banning anti-personnel mines.[116] Other than the permissive provisions of the Vienna Convention there appears to be no specific basis in international law for the function of public diplomacy itself.

6.5 Conclusions

There appears to be something of a lacuna in public international law as far as public diplomacy is concerned. Diplomatic practice stems from state sovereignty – the current articulation of which is the United Nations Charter – and has developed over time in response to wider changes in international society. Article 3 of the Vienna Convention allows states to exercise considerable discretion in public diplomacy activity – subject to the provisions of Article 41. This discretion is regulated – to the extent it is regulated at all – by reciprocity and mutual advantage.

113   Jan Melissen, *Beyond the New Public Diplomacy*, Netherlands Institute of International Relations "Clingendael", 2011, Number 3: http://www.clingendael.nl/publications/2011/20111014_cdsp_paper_jmelissen.pdf (Retrieved August 2015).

114   It is instructive to consider the debate about Internet freedom, where the United States and China find themselves at opposite ends of the spectrum. See, for example, Monroe E. Price, *The Battle over Internet Regulatory Paradigms: an Intensifying Area for Public Diplomacy*, USC Center on Public Diplomacy, 3 August 2010: http://uscpublicdiplomacy.org/index.php/newswire/cpdblog_detail/the_battle_over_internet_regulatory_paradigms_an_intensifying_area_for/ (Retrieved August 2015).

115   Jan Melissen, 2011.

116   See, for example, Shirley V Scott and Luciana Orana, *International Law, Soft Power and Public Diplomacy*, Australian National University College of Law, 2011: https://research.unsw.edu.au/people/associate-professor-shirley-veronica-scott/publications?type=conferencepapers (Retrieved August 2015).

PART 2
PUBLIC DIPLOMACY: HOW TO DO IT

Chapter 7

Tools and Techniques of Public Diplomacy

Exhibit Opening
UN Photo/Eskinder Debebe

7.1 Introduction

In Part 1, we considered definitions of public diplomacy and the changing environment in which it is practised. In Part 2, we shall be examining the tools and techniques available to practitioners of public diplomacy.

A central principle of public diplomacy is that it involves listening to target audiences as well as sending them a message. In looking at the techniques of public diplomacy, we shall bear in mind the context in which they are most likely to be employed.

We shall look first at traditional tools: cultural and educational exchange, training, seminars and conferences, exhibitions, missions, sponsored visits, broadcasting, speeches, and managing relations with the media. We shall then consider briefly more recent techniques driven by the development of new technologies. These are examined in more detail in Chapter 11.

7.2 Cultural and educational exchange

As we have already seen, cultural exchange is intrinsically devoid of any overt political message. But the richness of a nation's culture conveys a positive impression, whether in the form of high culture (characterised by art, opera or classical dance) or in its "low" form (such as sport, popular music or fashion). Governments therefore encourage, and frequently subsidise, such exchanges, at which point we begin to talk about cultural diplomacy. Governments often give assistance to young and relatively unknown artists, so as to demonstrate their commitment to new and innovative talent. They also, however, strongly encourage big-ticket events, such as a performance by a celebrated musician, or a major exhibition illustrating their country's history and culture.[117]

Another fruitful area for exchange is in the academic field, both in the sciences and the humanities.

Educational exchanges more broadly, and scholarship programmes in particular, have a special value, because they involve young people and therefore represent an investment in the future. Some scholarships are based on altruism and aimed at encouraging development, both of the individual scholars and their countries of origin. Others, less selflessly, are designed to cultivate leaders of the future. The problem with such schemes is that their effects are long-term, so that success is difficult to predict or measure. Consequently, when governments are strapped for cash, scholarship budgets frequently suffer. In the absence of a specific political message in cultural and educational exchanges, there is an argument, in terms of enhancing their credibility, for putting some distance between them and the governments themselves. The existence of autonomous cultural institutions such as the Alliance Française, the British Council and the Goethe Institute allows for such distance, which helps account for the success and reputation of these institutions.

---

117   As we noted in Chapter 3, major sporting events such as the Olympic games also provide an opportunity for the host nation to promote its national image.

Another activity worth mentioning under the broad heading of cultural exchange is "town-twinning". Encouraged by governments, but essentially driven by decisions at municipal level, town-twinning – alongside exchange visits – played an important role in bringing together the peoples of Europe after the Second World War. It has now become a global phenomenon.[118]

7.3 Training

At first sight, training people from other countries is quite clearly "messaging", in that its essence is instruction. Whether they come from the armed forces, the police, the civil service, NGOs, business, trades unions or academic and professional institutions, the role of trainers is to impart skills and experience. Nevertheless, training is also akin to educational exchange, building long-term relationships in addition to the immediate benefits to the global commons such training may create.

7.4 Seminars and conferences

Seminars and conferences can sit at virtually any point in the listening-messaging spectrum. Think tanks and similar institutions around the world – including many sponsored by governments[119] – organize discussions on issues of global concern, such as climate change and human rights, or intractable regional issues such as the dispute between Israel and the Palestinians. In doing so, they allow many voices to be heard that might otherwise not have the opportunity.

At the other end of the spectrum, governments arrange seminars to encourage trade, inward investment and tourism. While frequently making a nod towards the central principle of public relations by involving contributions from satisfied customers, these events are most definitely in "messaging" mode.

How effective are such events, aside from providing an opportunity to develop personal relationships? By their nature, conferences aimed at facilitation are difficult to judge. Even if there is an improvement in the problem under discussion, it is not easy to attribute this exclusively to the relevant event, even if it may have made a contribution. It is easier to judge the success of a hard-sell event if there is a notable increase in trade, investment or tourism in the subsequent period (although even then one must be wary of confusing correlation with causation). We shall be considering the problems of evaluation in Chapter 14.

118   See European Twinning: http://www.twinning.org/en/ (Retrieved August 2015).
119   An example of such an institution is Wilton Park, an agency of the British Foreign and Commonwealth Office. A history of Wilton Park describes it as follows: "Its aim was and is to unite people: to bring together those who disagree, often violently, and by patient, outspoken discussion of their conflicting views and assumptions, to reconcile rivals and enemies in recognition of their common humanity, their shared problems and their joint hopes of peace." See: http://www.wiltonpark.org.uk/en/ (Retrieved August 2015).

7.5 Exhibitions

Exhibitions can also fit into the Fisher/Bröckerhoff[120] spectrum at many places. Where the focus is cultural, the messaging is relatively muted, although cultural exhibitions can be effective in burnishing national image[121]. Where the focus is commercial, the messaging is far more direct. Most companies participate in trade fairs entirely independently. However, many governments provide financial and other assistance to exhibiting companies, particularly small and medium enterprises, and frequently have stands of their own promoting inward investment or tourism.

In a special category for messaging are world fairs. Participating countries vie with each other to demonstrate their commercial and scientific prowess. For the host nation the fair is both a major organisational challenge and an opportunity to impress. Privately, many governments may doubt the positive return they receive for the high investment involved, but few have the nerve to opt out of the process.

7.6 Missions

Outward and inward missions are a staple component of trade and investment promotion and are undoubtedly about messaging, but equally entail listening. Their objective is to build bridges between buyers and sellers and between potential investment partners. Export-oriented missions are normally organised by trade associations or chambers of commerce, but governments often provide assistance and sometimes take the lead, particularly in relatively difficult markets where political access is important. Inward investment promotion missions are led by governments, although frequently devolved to a specialised agency.

Inward missions in areas other than trade and investment promotion, when paid for by governments, fall into the category of sponsored visits (see below).

7.7 Sponsored visits

Sponsored visits are a highly effective way of conveying a message. Visitors are closely targeted by virtue of their role and expected influence, whether they be politicians, government officials, businessmen, academics, trades unionists, media representatives or members of civil society. Their programme will focus on a particular issue of interest to the host government, but at the same time they will be exposed to the country's wider political, economic and cultural environment. If the visit is intelligently conceived, there will also be scope for listening.

120   Ali Fisher and Aurélie Bröckerhoff, *Options for Influence*, Berkeley, Counterpoint, 2008.
121   A typical example of such an exhibition is Turks: A Journey of a Thousand Years, 600-1600 AD, held at the Royal Academy of Arts in London (and elsewhere) in 2005.

While there may be less evidence of immediate return than in the case of, for example, training, visits are less problematic in terms of judging outcomes than scholarship-financed study. This is not to say that scholarships are not very important in building long-term relationships. It is simply that visits are likely to offer more evidence of short-term gain.

7.8 Broadcasting

The advent of radio and television put far-reaching tools for messaging into the hands of governments. We have already seen how radio played a powerful role in wartime and during the Cold War. Since 9/11 much has been invested by many countries in radio and television broadcasting. The Qatar-based Al Jazeera (launched in the previous decade) has come to particular prominence in this period.

The problem with broadcasting is that, the closer governments are involved, the more suspicious the audience becomes that its product is propaganda. This suspicion is in some cases well-founded.

One broadcasting organisation with a particular reputation for objectivity and lack of bias is the BBC World Service. Operating under an independent charter since its inception, the BBC acquired its reputation for accurate reporting during the Second World War, and seeks to uphold that reputation at all times. Even the BBC, however, is viewed in some countries as an agent of the British Government.[122]

7.9 Speeches

The speech is the oldest tool of public diplomacy and retains great power as a means of conveying a message. Even though messages are invariably amplified and disseminated through other media outlets, either traditional or new, they frequently have their origin in speeches.

Sometimes speeches are free-standing, sometimes they are made in the context of a conference or other major event. What they have in common is that, with very few exceptions, they are made in the first instance to a live audience. We shall be examining the techniques involved in speech-making in Lesson 8.

7.10 Managing relations with the media

In dealing with the traditional media (press, radio and television), governments are clearly in "messaging" mode. Governments want accurate and positive coverage of their policies and behaviour and, to this end, send a constant stream of messages to the media. Concerned for their electoral future, governments also pay close attention to what the media have to say, and are quick to try to rectify any inaccuracies.

---

122   The BBC have in recent years experienced particular difficulty in Iran (see: http://edition.cnn.com/2009/WORLD/meast/01/21/iran.bbc.persian/index.html?iref=24hours) and China (see: http://www.zdnet.com/article/bbc-hits-out-at-chinese-broadcast-blocks) (Retrieved August 2015).

In the practice of public diplomacy, governments principally deal with foreign media through two main channels: diplomatic missions overseas and correspondents in the home capital (but see below on the use of the Internet). For many countries, the scope of the latter is limited by the level of representation of the foreign media. Where cities are major media centres, such as Washington, Paris or London, dealing with foreign correspondents is an extremely effective way of getting the message across.

The various techniques involved in dealing with the media are examined in more detail in Chapter 9.

7.11 More recent techniques: use of the Internet and social media; mobile telephones

The Internet has become so much part of our everyday lives that it is difficult to believe that twenty years ago the World Wide Web, which opened up the Internet to private consumers, had only just been invented.[123] Today, any organisation of note has a website, use of e-mail is universal, and social networks are widely used. Use of mobile phones has also grown exponentially, while the technologies of the phone and the Internet have converged to allow users, wherever they may be located, perpetual contact with their networks.

These developments present enormous challenges to governments, but they also offer opportunities for widespread dissemination of their messages, for segmented targeting and for at least a degree of interaction – involving listening – with their audiences. We shall look at the techniques involved in the use of digital technologies in Chapter 10.

7.12 Conclusions

There is a wide range of techniques employed in the practice of public diplomacy, most of them extremely venerable, some still in their infancy. Some of these techniques are better suited to messaging than listening, but this is not invariably so. We shall now be looking in more detail at specific techniques related to speech-making and dealing with the media, before looking at how to construct an effective public diplomacy campaign.

---

123   For a brief history of the Internet, see: http://www.internetsociety.org/internet/internet-51/history-internet/brief-history-internet (Retrieved August 2015).

Chapter 8

Speech-making

Interpreter translating speaker's remarks
UN Photo/TW

8.1 Introduction

Most people find themselves making a speech at some stage in their life, if only at a wedding or an office-leaving party. For diplomats, however, whether or not they are specialising in public diplomacy work, the incidence of public speaking – or preparing speeches for others to deliver – is likely to be greater than the average.

The key to a successful speech is very simple: your audience must enjoy listening to you. This means that you must be telling them something they did not know already, or offering them a fresh insight into something of which they already have knowledge. It also means that your speech should be constructed, and delivered, in such a way as to keep the audience engaged. Ideally, they should be stimulated and entertained: at a minimum, they must never be bored.

The circumstances surrounding each speech will, of course, vary considerably. Welcoming people to a dinner party – or making an after-dinner speech – is, for example, different from talking to an audience of university students or journalists about matters of high policy. The keynote speech at a seminar on investment calls for a very different register from that required in a tribute at a memorial service. Similarly, a speech to the United Nations General Assembly requires an approach other than that deployed at a National Day reception.

Despite these differences, adhering to certain essential principles can contribute to the success or otherwise of a speech. In this chapter we shall look at these principles and the related techniques we can employ, both in writing a speech and in delivering it. But before writing we need to prepare.

8.2 Preparation

"Time spent in reconnaissance is never wasted." [124]

Before embarking on writing a speech, it is important to establish a number of things. The two essential questions one should ask are:

1. What message do you wish to convey?
2. To whom are you speaking?

1. The message

It might seem obvious to state that you need to know the message of your speech. However, speakers can sometimes get caught up in multiple messages, which their audience find difficult to digest. Let us say, for example, that you are serving in your embassy overseas and have been invited to talk to a group of local university students about the role of the United Nations in the 21st Century. This is a subject you could talk about for many hours, but in fact – in this imaginary case – you have only thirty

---

124   Variously attributed to George Washington, Clausewitz, Napoleon and General Custer, and generally accepted as true by armed forces everywhere.

minutes. What message do you wish to convey in the time available? Is your government strongly in favour of UN reform? Are human rights your first priority? Or sustainable development? Or something else entirely? Whatever is the case you must keep the message always at the centre of your mind during the writing of the speech. You may well want to say several different things, which is fine, as long as you do not lose sight of the essential question: why have you agreed to make this speech? What message, above all, do you want the audience to take away at the end? (It may help focus your mind – and that of your audience – to build your message into the title of the speech.)

2. The audience

You want to know as much as possible about your audience (age, gender, ethnic and religious composition, education and professional experience and so on), so that you can tailor your speech accordingly. Above all, if you are to avoid the extreme vices of either boring your audience or leaving them stranded in a fog of non-comprehension, you must have a good understanding of what they already know about the subject. In the case above, you would at least need to know, for example, whether the students were studying international relations. If so, you could assume at least basic knowledge on their part of the work of the United Nations.

It is also important to know how many people there will be in the audience. You cannot, for example, give a formal speech to a round table of a dozen people – you would want to speak extempore, using notes. It is more likely, however, that you would be talking to a group of around forty or so, in which case you would probably be better off using a script, particularly if you are operating in a foreign language. If you find yourself facing a hall filled with a hundred or more people, you will need to be prepared to use a microphone, which has an inevitable distancing effect.

There are other things it is also important to know:

3. Length of the speech

If you are asked to speak for five minutes or less, you self-evidently cannot cover as much ground as you could in thirty or forty minutes. Your safest bet is therefore to settle for one major issue and deal with it in reasonable depth. If you insist on including every issue you would ideally like to cover, you will wind up with a relatively meaningless catalogue of points.

4. Other speakers

Are there other speakers? If so, what ground will they be covering, and what is the running order? You will want to avoid overlap – particularly if you are speaking later. If possible, you should make direct contact with the other speakers in advance in order to compare notes.

5. The venue

Where and what is the venue? Does it have a lectern (strongly recommended) or the necessary equipment if you are planning to use visual aids? And will you have the opportunity for reconnaissance?

8.3 Writing the speech

1. Structure

All speeches should have a clear structure. This is true of any communication of length, but it is particularly important in a speech, because it is occurring in real time. You are effectively taking your audience on a journey and you need to make life as easy as possible for them by telling them where they are going, where they are at any point in the journey, and when they have arrived.

At the very least, therefore, all speeches – however short – should have a beginning, a middle, and an end. The beginning should be used to introduce the subject to your audience and provide them with a road map to the rest of the speech; the middle is the section with the bulk of the content; and the end is where you draw final conclusions.

You should write the middle section first, i.e. the body of the speech. Until you have this section the way you want it, you cannot sensibly write either the introduction or the conclusion.

2. Body of the speech

At the beginning of the speech-writing process, it sometimes makes sense to brainstorm and get down on paper, uncritically, as many points as possible that you might wish to include in your speech. These points can then be refined, prioritised or discarded as you construct the speech. You will also need to conduct research to fill the gaps in your knowledge that the process has revealed.

It is very important that the body of the speech itself should also have its own internal structure, so that the audience may clearly grasp the various points you are making. Unless you have a clear structure there is a danger, when you have a large number of points to make, either that your speech will turn into a narrated list or that you will ramble from one point to another.

As a general rule, it makes sense to divide the body of your speech into three main sections (but be flexible: you can have more, or less, as necessary). If, as is usually the case, you have a larger number of points you wish to make, then these should be grouped within your three main sections.

If we take, for example, the aforementioned speech about the United Nations, you might want to talk about all of the following points:

- The Security Council veto;
- Developing countries' representation in the Security Council;
- Responsibility to Protect (R2P);
- The Millennium Development Goals;
- The workings of the Human Rights Council;
- The effectiveness of the UNDP.

Depending on your main message (see above), you could group these points as follows:

i.   Institutional questions

- The Security Council veto;
- Developing countries' representation in the Security Council;
- The workings of the Human Rights Council.

ii.   Development issues

- The Millennium Development Goals;
- The effectiveness of the UNDP.

iii. Major philosophical challenges

- R2P.

This is not, of course, the only way in which you could order these subjects. It is the principle that is important: always have a clear structure, so that your audience never has to work too hard to grasp your message.

Once you have written the body of the speech you can then turn to drafting the introduction and conclusion.

3. The introduction

The introduction to the speech is the moment you want to get your audience to sit up and pay attention. If you lose their interest at this stage, chances are you may never get it back. So, be bold and, if necessary, provocative. Depending on the nature of the speech – and your audience – you could open with a joke. But be careful with jokes, because they do not always traverse cultural and linguistic boundaries with ease. A safer alternative is a quotation which will pave the way for the rest of the speech, or perhaps a personal anecdote of relevance, or possibly a question you might ask your audience to be pondering during your speech.

In the example of the United Nations speech, you could consider using the following quotation from Kofi Annan, when, as Secretary-General, he presented the Millennium Report to the General Assembly:

> "We are at the service of the world's peoples, and we must listen to them. They are telling us that our past achievements are not enough. They are telling us we must do more, and do it better." [125]

Having whetted your audience's appetite, you should then tell them how you plan to deal with your subject, by saying something along the following lines:

> "Fifteen years on from the publishing of the Millennium Report, it is worth asking ourselves: how much progress has been made and how might we do better in the future?"

---

125   Kofi Annan, speech to the United Nations General Assembly, New York, 3 April 2000.

"In addressing these questions today, I'll be starting by looking at some institutional issues (and particularly, within that context, the workings of the UNSC and the Human Rights Council). Then I'll be considering the development challenges, including the role of the UNDP. And finally I want to discuss the major current philosophical challenge, which is R2P, before offering some personal conclusions of my own."

Your audience will now know exactly where you are planning to take them – but not, of course, the detail of what you will be saying.

4. The conclusion

Many speeches just seem to peter out, as though the speaker had run out of ideas or energy. To avoid this impression, you need a strong conclusion. This should be consistent with what you have said in the body of the speech, but you should avoid simply repeating what you have already said. Best of all is if you can offer a forceful and persuasive conclusion that grants a fresh insight while resting firmly on what has gone before. A final, ringing, quotation also never goes amiss.

In the case of the United Nations speech, you might, for example, say something like:

"As will be clear from what I have been saying, there is enormous change under way in the United Nations."

"Change is never easy and, for reasons I have already rehearsed, some change is very difficult indeed."

"Given the circumstances surrounding all the issues I have discussed today, my own view is that the main focus for our efforts in the immediate future should be [your choice]."

"It is here that change is both desperately needed and, given the political will, entirely feasible in a relatively short space of time."

"To encourage us all in this great endeavour I leave with you the words of [your choice of quotation]."

5. Signposts

The road map in your introduction has told your audience broadly speaking where you are planning to take them. Equally important, however, are the road signs you provide along the way to ensure that they do not get lost. Every time you move on to another part of your speech, you must let the audience know what you are doing. This is easily and naturally done by using, for example, the following kind of linking sentences:

"Let us begin then with the institutional questions, and first of all with the Security Council...."

"So much for the Security Council. What then of the Human Rights Council?"

"Let us move now from institutional matters to the all-important question of development..."

...and so on.

In this manner, you will keep your audience alongside you on your journey and not leave them, confused and irritated, by the wayside.

6. Language

In speech-making, simplest is often best. A speech is not a dissertation or a chapter of a book. It is a real-time communication, in which all possible barriers to comprehension should be stripped away. Keep your sentences – and paragraphs – in general short, but of variable length. Practise making the speech before actually delivering it, or before passing it on to the person for whom it has been written. You will soon identify the awkward rhythms that need to be eliminated.

8.4 Delivering the speech

There is very little that an excellent delivery can do to make a badly written speech sound good (despite the no doubt apocryphal story of the clergyman who would write "Shout like hell!" in the margin next to the weakest part of his Sunday sermon).

However, it is entirely possible to ruin a well-written speech through bad delivery. Here are ten golden rules that will help avoid this:

i.   Before you go on, do breathing exercises: this will both calm you down and get the adrenaline flowing;

ii.   Pause before you begin speaking, to allow the audience to settle;

iii. Speak slowly – and maintain an even pace (many speakers begin well, but degenerate into a gabble as they progress through their speech);

iv.   Speak clearly;

v.   Vary your volume and tone, according to the significance of what you are saying, but make sure that you are always audible;

vi.   Use pauses for dramatic effect;

vii. Maintain good eye contact with your audience (this can be difficult when you are reading a script, but it will come with practice: move your gaze from side to side and from the front to the back so that everyone in the audience feels engaged in the speech process);

viii. Avoid gesticulating wildly, but do not be afraid to make hand gestures to emphasise particular points;

ix.   Do not exceed your time limit. No-one will mind if you run a few minutes under;

x.   Above all, engage with your audience, communicating to them your enthusiasm for the subject and letting them see your personality shining through the words you speak.

8.5 Speech template

Below is a speech template based on what we have been discussing in this chapter. You can vary it according to particular circumstances.

INTRODUCTION

A striking statement, joke or quotation

Explanation of the scope and structure of the speech

BODY OF SPEECH

Lead in

Point 1

Linking sentence

Point 2

Linking sentence

Point 3

CONCLUSION

Lead in

Concluding Remarks

Final statement, joke or quotation

Chapter 9

Dealing with the Media

Speaking to the press
UN Photo/Jean-Marc Ferré

9.1 Introduction

As we saw in Chapter 4, governments have had to contend with the media for two hundred years or more. When governments had a near-monopoly on information about events in the international realm, they were able to tell the media more or less what they wanted, when they wanted. Those days are long gone.

In terms of news dissemination, the traditional media outlets (the press, radio and television) are themselves under threat from the new forms of media, which can effectively by-pass them in spreading information over vast informal international networks. However, the traditional media are still immensely influential, and are embracing the new technologies in a bid to remain so.

Governments have therefore had to adapt to a world of 24-hour news coverage, with perpetual demand for immediate comment on events as they unfold. Difficult as this makes policy-making – it is now unthinkable to seek to make policy without taking into account how it will play in the media – this also provides opportunities for those who are well-prepared to convey desired messages in timely fashion to particular audiences.

9.2 Cultivating the media

Getting messages into the media is not, however, simply a matter of providing carefully crafted copy – essential though this is, as no one is interested in a dull product. There is a range of techniques that can be deployed according to circumstances: these are discussed below. A good public diplomacy official will be cultivating a relationship with key media contacts on a regular basis to ensure that the necessary channels are open when they are required. This is applicable both to officers serving in foreign ministries, or at organisation headquarters, and to those posted in embassies in the field. It may be necessary, and advantageous, to give selected journalists background briefing (see below).

It is worth remembering that journalists are under enormous pressure to produce a story, and to be the first to do so. Helping them will help you get the story out accurately.

The following essential precepts for dealing with the media are based on suggestions by Richard Halloran, former foreign and military correspondent of the New York Times. They should be born in mind during the course of this lesson:

i.   Project a professional and civil attitude, neither pandering to the press nor evincing hostility.
ii.   Understand that there is no such institution as "the media." The press, television, and radio are diverse and competitive. The biggest difference is between print and broadcast: print reporters need time and explanation, while broadcasters need pictures and sound bites.
iii.   Learn the ground rules: know what is on the record, what is not for attribution and what is off the record (i.e., not for public use). The safest rule is always to tell a journalist only what you want to see in the newspaper or on the air.
iv.   Lying to the press is never permissible.

v.   Discuss only matters pertinent to your nation or organisation. Never speculate or answer a hypothetical question.

vi.   Don't wait for the news to happen. Always be ready to respond. Assume that leaks will occur.

vii.   Never let a mistake stand: uncorrected mistakes acquire a life of their own.[126]

9.3 Press releases

The press release is the standard form of communication with the media. It can contain a statement of significance (see "statements" below) or can simply convey information of a routine nature. It might, for example, relate to an ambassadorial appointment, a ministerial visit, a forthcoming conference or any other event, past, present or future, to which you might wish to draw public attention. Unless the subject is clearly of minor interest, press releases are normally distributed widely to the media at large. These days they will usually be distributed by e-mail and will also appear immediately on a foreign ministry or other government website.

The key to a good press release is to avoid excessive length, to get the main message in the opening sentences and to employ language that journalists can use directly, or easily adapt. Depending on the subject, there should be illustrative material (photographs, video and so on) to support the text, as well as detailed background information. The easier you can make life for the media, the more likely it is that your message will be conveyed in full.

Press releases normally carry an embargo to ensure that information is not prematurely released.

A typical routine press release might read as follows:

"APPOINTMENT OF NEW RURITANIAN AMBASSADOR TO LILLIPUT

0900 Local Time, 1 July 2015 Ruritania City*

Mr Wolfgang Mozart has been appointed Ruritanian Ambassador in Lilliput City in succession to Mr Giuseppe Verdi, who will be taking up another diplomatic appointment elsewhere.

Mr Mozart, who takes up his appointment in February, was formerly Ambassador in Brobdignag City and has previously served in [etc etc]. He will be accompanied by his wife and two children.

ENDS

Contact: [contact details of press officer responsible]"

*i.e., the release is embargoed until then. The press release would probably also include a detailed biographical note on the new ambassador.

---

126   Richard Halloran, 2007.

9.4 Statements

Sometimes press releases will contain statements of significance, designed to convey a clear message to the world about a government's position on a particular issue.

Depending on the nature of the subject, the statement may be in the name of the government, or of the foreign minister personally (or another minister), or of the head of government.

If the subject is sufficiently important, the statement will be linked to a public appearance by a senior member of the government. He or she will use the language of the statement as the basis for an interview, allowing them to enlarge on the government's position. An edited video clip of this interview will be published on the relevant government website and trailed via social media outlets.

Statements are frequently – though not invariably – made in response to urgent developments and therefore designed for immediate publication.

The body of a press release containing a typical – if somewhat extreme – statement might read as follows:

"The Ruritanian Government views with deep concern the widespread civil unrest in Brobdignag, which has given rise to a number of tragic deaths. It urges the *Brobdig*nag Government to exercise maximum restraint in its efforts to restore order and to respect the demonstrators' legitimate right of protest. Ruritania will continue to monitor the situation closely and reserves the right to take appropriate action in the event of serious human rights abuses."

9.5 Briefings

A press briefing is something less than a press conference (see below), but provides an opportunity to amplify the information provided in press releases in a way that will allow journalists to write a more interesting story.

Briefings may be conducted on an individual basis with trusted journalists, who may be given access to experts on specialised subjects or topics of current interest. In this case, it is important to establish the ground rules about sources. While it is frequently helpful to get information into the public domain without attribution, there are clearly dangers in this practice.[127] Even more difficult is the notion of providing background material for information only. As Halloran has argued, it is best not to say anything to a journalist you would not wish to see published.[128]

Alternatively, a press briefing can be totally transparent and open to all. In light of twenty-four hour news coverage, many foreign ministries have now abandoned what was once the standard practice of a daily

---

127   The author once gave information to a journalist in an unnamed country on the strict understanding that it was unattributable. The journalist published the story as a direct quotation from a [fictitious] document allegedly leaked from the author's embassy. When remonstrated with, the journalist defended his action by saying that he had not mentioned the author's actual name.
128   Richard Halloran, 2007.

press briefing, when announcements were made at a set time and responses given to questions by a press spokesperson. Among others, however, the US State Department continues this daily practice in briefings that are videoed and can be seen on the Department's website.[129]

9.6 Signed articles

An article placed in leading newspapers, signed by an ambassador, foreign minister or head of government, can be an effective vehicle for conveying a message about a particular policy or relationship. Such articles work particularly well if timed to coincide with a visit to a country or region by the signatory. If relations with the country being visited allow, and if there is sufficient congruence of opinion on policy issues, a joint article between, for example, the foreign ministers or the heads of government of the two countries can convey the message even more powerfully.

9.7 Speeches

As we have seen in Chapter 8, speeches have been used since time immemorial to inform and influence publics. The Internet can today be used to disseminate speeches by text and video directly to a very wide audience. Nevertheless, media coverage remains extremely important. The texts of significant speeches are usually released in advance, with a suitable embargo and a warning that the authoritative version will be that actually delivered on the day. This means that, even if there are some adjustments to the final text, journalists will have the opportunity to prepare their commentary in good time for publication as soon as the speech is delivered.

As in the case of press conferences (see below), the media will normally also be given a complete kit related to the speech, containing background material, photographs and contact details.

9.8 Press conferences

Press conferences invariably accompany any significant event and provide an opportunity to combine a statement with a question-and-answer session. Press conferences need to be carefully stage-managed to ensure that all the journalists attending feel satisfied that they have had the opportunity to put their questions. A substantial amount of background material will be supplied in media kits, but journalists will always be looking for an original angle in their portrayal.

In the case of a visit to another country by, say, a foreign minister, his embassy will need to decide on whether the press conference should be held independently or jointly with the hosting minister. There

---

129   See the State Department website: http://www.state.gov/ (Retrieved August 2015).

are obvious advantages to the latter arrangement. If feasible, the more the two ministers are able to speak in harmony, the stronger the impression of a successful and productive visit. Furthermore, for a busy embassy, there is an administrative gain in that the host government would be responsible for the logistics. On the other hand, there might be a particular aspect of the visit (say, to encourage inward investment) that the visiting minister would wish to stress. In that case, a separate, additional press conference could be held at the embassy.

9.9 Interviews

In Chapter 12 we shall be discussing the art of being interviewed. The point of an individual interview is to permit a journalist to ask more detailed questions than might be possible in an open forum. In turn, this will allow the interviewee to convey his/her message clearly to a particular audience, i.e. the readers or viewers of the media outlet concerned. This entails judicious selection of appropriate media according to the likely subjects to be discussed, and clearly understood ground rules about the questions to be posed.

Interviews may follow on immediately after a press conference or they may be arranged independently, according to convenience.

9.10 Group discussions

There are many news magazine programmes on television and radio where the favoured format is a group discussion involving representatives of differing points of view. This can provide an excellent opportunity for a politician or diplomat to advocate a policy or opinion, but it clearly has its dangers. It is one thing to have to contend with a single interviewer, but a group discussion in real time presents rather more complex problems. Participants need to be supremely confident of their position in case they find themselves under fire from several different directions at once.

9.11 Hospitality

In many countries the relationship between governments and the media has become a sensitive issue, with serious concerns arising when that relationship appears to be too close – or when excessive hospitality is involved – leading in extreme cases to the possibility of corruption. At the same time, governments clearly cannot isolate themselves entirely from the media, so a balance needs to be established. At press conferences, some form of modest refreshment is normally served. Press officers may find it convenient to meet a trusted journalist over a drink or a reasonably priced lunch. Inward visits to allow journalists to see for themselves what is going on in your country, or fellowships to allow them to conduct research, are sensible and constructive ways of fostering the relationship.

9.12 Crisis management

When a crisis occurs, such as a kidnapping or the outbreak of serious conflict, foreign ministries put emergency machinery into operation. A media unit is essential to the successful management of the crisis.

The golden rule in a crisis is to provide the media with an immediate and credible story. Otherwise, they will look elsewhere for facts and may construct a story that is unhelpful to your cause. This is rarely an easy thing to achieve: by their nature, crises evolve rapidly and there will be much genuine uncertainty, both about the facts and about how your government, or organisation, will react. Nevertheless, there is no excuse for saying nothing. The key is to be honest about the situation: tell the media what you can, explain your difficulties and promise to tell them more as soon as you are able to. Most importantly, keep that promise.

A core difficulty, as explained by Jamie O'Shea, a former NATO spokesman, is the gap between the perspectives of governments and the media. Governments, who have an absolute duty to the truth, tend to offer intellectual arguments and to contemplate the long term. The media, on the other hand, deal in pictures, emotions, and on-the-ground realities.

O'Shea's essential principles for dealing with this difficulty are threefold:

i.   Information: give the media as much accurate, honest and reliable information as you can, so that you become a credible source of opinion.
ii. Coordination: avoid contradictory statements from different parts of the organisation; speed is important, but accuracy and consistency are even more so.
iii. Anticipation: stories have to be prepared in advance so that they can be released without delay when the right moment comes.

In support of these principles, O'Shea identifies six key tasks. Crisis managers should:

i.   Establish a 24-hour media centre;
ii. Monitor the media to identify weaknesses and opportunities in their position;
iii. Plan each day on a controlled theme: a speech, a briefing, synchronised "op ed" pieces and so on.
iv. Focus on the appropriate media market;
v.   Prepare rebuttals (propaganda does not kill itself – see also Halloran above);
vi. Energise the whole organisation at all levels of the chain of command, so that the crisis is seen as being managed.[130]

---

130   Jamie O'Shea, *Public Diplomacy: Managing a Crisis*, International Diplomatic Training Forum, Bruges, 24 September, 2008.

9.13 Press lines

As we have seen above, successful media management requires forward planning, coordination and discipline. It is essential that all parties involved, whether in the foreign ministry (or other organisation headquarters) or in overseas embassies, are speaking from the same script. This means that an agreed line to take on any given issue should be disseminated in timely fashion throughout the system in order to ensure consistency on the part of all those concerned.

9.14 Conclusions

Despite the rapid growth of new media (use of which we shall be examining in Chapter 10), managing relations with the traditional media remains an essential component of creating and implementing foreign policy. In Chapter 11 we shall be exploring how to design a media plan employing the techniques discussed above. In Chapter 12 we shall consider how to behave when being interviewed by the media.

Chapter 10

TWEETS	FOLLOWING	FOLLOWERS	LISTS
20.1K	202	6.49M	6

Use of Digital Technologies

Except of the White House's Twitter account profile
July 2015

10.1 Introduction

As we saw in Chapter 5, governments have to contend with an increasingly connected world in which they have long lost their once near-monopoly on information in the international realm. Digital technologies, and related societal change, present a serious challenge to diplomacy. However, they also offer opportunities, which we shall be exploring in this chapter.

10.2 Private sector use of digital technologies

In the private sector, the proliferation of digital channels and technologies has enabled a level of dialogue and interaction between brands and consumers never reached before.

While traditional methods of marketing and brand management meant a more passive consumption of messages by the consumer, digital technologies have changed the ways in which businesses can engage with their audiences and customers.

Online media, such as search listings and display advertising (both on the web and mobile phones), can be used to drive potential customers towards specific websites. Messages to customers can be tailored, based, for example, on previous behaviour, interests, and demographic data. Tracking allows companies to calculate the direct return on their advertising investment and to ensure activity is continually optimised in order to improve performance. E-mail campaigns can reach large numbers of potential customers far more economically, and with greater precision, than old-style mail shots.

Equally, technology has empowered consumers in the ways in which they can engage with brands, and talk about them online. And social networking sites allow companies to join in the conversation with their customers on their own territory, as well as providing customer service within some of these channels. Finally, success can be judged against clear, quantitative objectives (such as increase in market share or revenues), linked in time to specific campaigns.

In short, successful businesses have happily embraced the networked world.

10.3 Governments and digital technologies

To what extent, and how successfully, can such uses of digital technology be applied by governments to their public diplomacy?

In a 2008 study, Nicholas Westcott, former Chief Information Officer at the Foreign and Commonwealth Office (FCO) in London, identified three crucial elements to successful exploitation of the Internet by governments: connection, presence and participation. Connection is a prerequisite, for without it there is no audience – and Internet penetration, while growing rapidly, remains very low in many parts of the world. Presence allows a government to be an actor. However, it is participation in the debate that brings genuine influence.[131]

10.4 Websites

The World Wide Web is only just over twenty years old, and yet today anyone and everyone with Internet access can have a website of their own. Websites are a basic marketing device, whether designed for individuals, the smallest of NGOs or the most powerful of multinational companies, terrorist groups, universities, trades unions, churches or entertainment venues.

Governments, and foreign ministries in particular, are no different from other users in this regard. But how successful have they been?

A perusal of a range of foreign ministry websites soon reveals considerable diversity. While many have at least nominally integrated the different forms of social media, some are in practice unattractive, static and inflexible offering little more than links to government statements and photographs of government ministers on overseas visits or receiving foreign dignitaries. At the other extreme, the best websites are being constantly refreshed, visually pleasing (and immediately identifiable), easy to use and offer a wide range of helpful links, both for their own citizens and for their potential target audiences overseas. Users of these websites can immediately see the views of the governments concerned on current international issues, and their foreign policy priorities. They can easily find their way to relevant speeches, statements (both in video and text) and other authoritative information. They are also invited to comment on blogs (for these foreign ministries, it is now routine for ministers and diplomats to blog[132]) and access a variety of links to other areas of the site or to relevant external sites. You Tube, Flickr, Facebook, Twitter and other social networks are offered as options for interaction. There are links to the governments' embassies overseas, whose own websites, while individual, conform to a recognisable standard and have clear and helpful links back to the foreign ministry's site – as well to those of other government departments and other relevant organisations.

Examples of the better websites are to be found, as is to be expected, among major developed countries, of which the United States is the supreme example.[133] A particular recent initiative of the State Department was the introduction on its website, in addition to existing blogging opportunities, of Opinion Space, which invited visitors to register their views on international issues, and to see where they stood on the opinion scale in relation to others in the world.[134]

---

131   Nicholas Westcott, *Digital Diplomacy: The Impact of the Internet on International Relations*, Oxford Internet Institute, Research Report, 16 July 2008.
132   The British Foreign and Commonwealth Office, for example, invites bloggers to participate in what it describes as "Global Conversations". See: http://blogs.fco.gov.uk/ (Retrieved August 2015).
133   http://www.state.gov/ (RetrievedAugust 2015).
134   This invitation is however no longer to be found on the State Department website. For information about the Opinion Space more generally see: http://opinion.berkeley.edu/ (RetrievedAugust 2015).

There are other impressive examples, which include – but are not limited to – the foreign ministry websites of Japan, South Korea and Brazil (although the latter is in Portuguese only). An example of an excellent website from a relatively small country is that of Singapore.[135]

It is important to underscore the fact that sustaining a successful website is resource-intensive. Setting it up is one thing, but making it effective, and ensuring that it is both up-to-date and evolving to keep pace with external developments, requires continuing financial, technical and human investment. Excellent and informative as many foreign ministry websites are, there remains the question of how to attract people to them in the first place. For international relations scholars, journalists or other government officials, accessing a foreign ministry website may seem like second nature. These are important audiences, but they by no means account for all the potential for influence using the Internet. For most people seeking an angle on what is going on in the world – other than what they may already have got from radio, television or the press – their first port of call is likely to be Google (or another search engine) or a social network of some description.

There are essentially two ways of having a website listed high up on Google (or other) pages. The first is to pay, which is effectively advertising and – some would argue – less relevant to a government operation. Of greater relevance to governments is the Search Engine Optimisation (SEO), namely making the website as authoritative and relevant as possible.[136]

Waiting for people to access a website, either direct or via a search engine, is the passive approach. The active approach is to go out to meet them in social networks.

10.5 Social networks

Social networks were originally conceived to be what their name suggests: a means of maintaining social contact between individuals in something close to real time. However, membership of such networks has rapidly become an absolute necessity for organisations of all kinds that wish to engage with their audiences, as broadly defined.

135   http://www.mofa.go.jp/
http://www.mofat.go.kr/ENG/main/index.jsp
http://www.itamaraty.gov.br/
http://www.mfa.gov.sg/content/mfa/index.html (All retrieved August 2015)
136   There are two ways of having a website listed high up on Google (or other search engines). Positions across the top and down the right hand side of the page are effectively paid advertising - see "pay per click" (PPC) below. The ten positions on the lower left are free of charge but determined by the search engines: these are known as organic or natural search listings, but can be influenced by search engine optimisation (SEO).
In PPC, advertisers bid on search terms (keywords) via an auction model for positions on the page, where cost is proportionate to the position (the advertiser only pays if the user clicks and visits the site). PPC also allows for rapid updating of messaging. PPC is more expensive than SEO but guarantees position.
SEO improves site position by making the website as authoritative and relevant as possible. This entails optimising the site structure and content, and by generating external commentary about the site. All these are taken into account by search engines when determining the site's position in their indexes for each keyword. While SEO incurs no payment to the search engine, it takes time and expertise and position is not guaranteed.

To understand why this should be, it is worth reminding ourselves of the statistics in Chapter 5. Facebook alone has 1.49 billion monthly active members, while Twitter has 316 million[137], numbers that are continually growing. Dominant as these networks undoubtedly are, there are many thousands more, big and small, linking people with particular interests across international boundaries.

Governments are no exception to this compulsion to join social networks. Over half the heads of state and government attending the G20 meeting in Seoul in 2010 were on Twitter – or more accurately, their staff were, in their name – although judging by the inconsequential content of their tweeting, professional diplomats need not fear for their jobs.[138] As we have seen above, many foreign ministries are making strenuous efforts to extend the reach of their websites by using, among others, Facebook, Twitter, Flickr and You Tube.

How can these networks be used constructively in public diplomacy? Facebook offers enormous opportunities for communication with large numbers of people, for targeting specific interest groups, and for engaging in constructive debate. Twitter is arguably handicapped in this respect by what many regard as its most admirable quality: the 140-character limit. There is no possibility of communicating anything but the simplest of messages via this route: the complex message behind the headline requires a further click of the mouse to an external link of some kind. This does not, however, deter ministers and ambassadors from tweeting, or on occasion, engaging in verbal combat.[139] And the obvious virtue of Twitter is that it operates as an alert mechanism and facilitates rapid dissemination of news in a fast-moving situation – one need only think of the Arab Spring.

As one might expect, the State Department – which, by one account, has 195 Twitter accounts, 288 Facebook accounts and 11 foreign-language Twitter feeds[140] – is a pioneer in the use of digital technologies in public diplomacy, although the effectiveness of its methods have still to be demonstrated. Much – though not all – of the work in this field has been driven recently by concern about American relations with the Islamic world. The Digital Outreach Team (DOT) at the State Department, while also on Facebook, You Tube, Flickr, and Twitter, seeks to talk directly to citizens in the Middle East, principally through posting messages about US foreign policy on popular Arabic, Urdu, and Persian language Internet forums. Their remit is to explain and to counter misinformation, not by simple messaging but by engaging in conversation. Unlike government bloggers from other countries, as a matter of principle DOT members, who are all native speakers of the languages of the forums, do not seek to conceal their official identity.[141]

137   http://newsroom.fb.com/company-info/ and
http://about.twitter.com/company (Both retrieved August 2015).
138   For an amusing account of how heads of state and government began to take to Twitter, see the talk given by Matthias Lüfkens of the World Economic Forum at the 2010 World Blogging Forum in Vienna: http://vimeo.com/17133654 (Retrieved August 2015).
139   *Ibid.*
140   Michele Keleman, *Twitter Diplomacy: State Department 2.0*, 21 February 2012: http://www.npr.org/blogs/alltechconsid-ered/2012/02/21/147207004/twitter-diplomacy-state-department-2-0 (Retrieved August 2015).
141   This practice goes against the views of those like Mark Leonard and Evgeny Morozov, who argue that such activities should be covert to maintain credibility. See: Mark Leonard, *Diplomacy by Other Means*, Foreign Policy, Number 132, Sept.-Oct. 2002, and Evgeny Morozov, *The Future of "Public Diplomacy 2.0". Net Effect*, Foreign Policy, 9 June 2009.

Judging by a case study based on Internet discussion following President Obama's speech in Cairo in 2009, the DOT has yet to demonstrate its success. Postings on forums after the DOT had joined the conversation (among which Al-Jazeera figured prominently) were even more negative about the United States than they had been previously. On the other hand, the DOT claim that their principal target is not the forum participants themselves, but "lurkers", for whom it is important to set the record straight (although there can be no way of judging the effectiveness of this).[142]

The State Department is tireless in its innovation: a Persian-language Google+ hangout has recently enabled the Department's spokesperson to answer questions from inside Iran delivered via prominent journalists.[143]

Other governments have sought to be innovative in different ways. The British Government, for example, has collaborated in the establishment of extranets to help move forward the global debate about climate change. (These are not public forums, a degree of restriction being felt necessary to ensure trusted participation.)[144]

One difficulty about the participation in social networks by governments is the tension between, on the one hand, the need for all their representatives to speak with one voice and, on the other, the democratic and open spirit of such networks. This is the old conundrum of hierarchy versus network, from which even private sector companies are not immune. It can only be resolved by constructing sensible overall guidelines and trusting staff to operate intelligently within them.

10.6 Mobile telephony

The exponential growth in mobile telephony and its integration with the Internet – which has enabled developing countries to leapfrog many of the ageing infrastructure issues of developed countries[145] – has brought great challenges to governments: video or photos of state violence or natural disaster captured on the spot by mobile phone can be on the Internet and around the world within seconds, long before governments can muster a public position. Opinions summarised in a text or e-mail can be disseminated just as fast. In turn, users have 24-hour access to information wherever they may be.

But can governments make use of this technology for their own purposes?

Governments certainly cannot afford to ignore it, and there is evidence that some governments are striving to make intelligent use of it.[146] Texting, for example (or messaging), is another way of driving target audiences towards specific websites. The relatively small size of mobile screens imposes

---

142   Lina Khatib, William Dutton and Michael Thelwall, *Public Diplomacy 2.0: An Exploratory Case Study of the US Digital Outreach Team*, CD-DRL Working Papers, 2011, Number 120: http://cddrl.stanford.edu/publications/public_diplomacy_20_an_exploratory_case_study_of_the_digi-tal_outreach_team (Retrieved August 2015) The study's overall conclusion is that the best way to change attitudes in the Middle East is via a foreign policy that matches words to deeds. But it also has some technical recommendations about, for example, the need to interpret and contextualise posted videos and texts, to respond more rapidly to negative blogging and to employ more visual images rather than, at present, largely logical rhetoric.
143   http://www.state.gov/documents/organization/189718.pdf (Retrieved August 2015).
144   Nicholas Westcott, 2008.
145   See, for example: http://blogs.hillandknowlton.com/hank/2012/02/24/the-rise-of-the-smartphone/ (Retrieved August 2015).
146   For example, the US State Department recently reported that more than 500,000 students in Tunisia have signed up for English language classes by mobile telephone. See: http://www.state.gov/documents/organization/189718.pdf (Retrieved August 2015).

inevitable limits to the complexity of the messages that can be delivered in this way (which appears to be more relevant to use in consular emergencies for example). But the rapid convergence of mobile telephone and Internet technologies has made it easy to access a wealth of information from a mobile phone. Governments and international organisations are becoming increasingly adept at modelling content in order to fit the smart phone/tablet format.[147]

10.7 Conclusions

Digital technologies are so much a part of everyday life that governments have no choice but to embrace them. Policy or ideological arguments may not actually be won or lost on the Internet, but it provides a medium for active exchange of ideas that cannot be ignored. The evidence indicates, however, that even the most advanced nations face a challenge in exploiting these technologies as effectively as business or civil society.

It is also worth remembering that social networks are not yet broadly adopted in all societies, suggesting that governments should not rush to abandon the more traditional means of communicating with foreign publics.[148]

Evaluating the success of public diplomacy on the Internet is also problematic. Businesses can set key performance indicators for advertising penetration and time-related increases in sales, both of which are precisely measurable. Governments seeking to judge their success in influencing the views of overseas publics are reliant on trends in opinion polls – the results of which may or may not be attributable to public diplomacy activities – or analysis of Internet forums – which does not reveal the views of "lurkers". There are sophisticated commercial services available to the private sector for monitoring and measuring sentiment in social media, but the number of governments systematically employing such services remains limited.[149]

We shall be examining the question of evaluation in public diplomacy more generally in Chapter 14.

---

147   See, for example, the arrangements for the 2012 Chicago NATO Summit: http://www.nato.int/chicago2012/mobile/ (Retrieved August 2015).

148   As is argued, for example, in James Glassman and Dan Dickman, Co-Chairs, *Strategic Public Diplomacy: The Case of Egypt*, Bipartisan Policy Center, October 2011.
Internet penetration in Afghanistan in 2013 was only 5.9% of the population. See: Internet World Stats: http://www.internetworldstats.com/asia/af.htm (Retrieved August 2015).

149   This does not mean however that some governments do not closely monitor social media and seek to exert censorship if they detect what they believe to be offensive or dangerous material. See, for example: http://www.theregister.co.uk/2012/05/20/pakistan_twitter_ban/ (Retrieved August 2015).

Chapter 11

Designing a Media Plan

UN Economic and Social Council (ECOSOC) holding a press conference
UN Photo/Rick Bajornas

11.1 Introduction

An essential component of any major organised event is media plan. Media coverage of crises occurs spontaneously. For a planned event, however, media attention needs to be generated.

In the case of a large-scale event, such as the Olympic games or a climate change summit, the logistics of media management are extremely complicated. For the purposes of this chapter we are going to focus on a more modest example, namely an overseas visit by a foreign minister. This is the kind of event with which readers of this book may well have to deal, and the principles involved are the same – however big the event – as are the techniques (which we examined in Chapter 9).

Imagine that you are responsible for press and public affairs at the Ruritanian Embassy in Lilliput City. Your Foreign Minister will shortly be paying a first working visit to Lilliput and wants to promote Ruritanian interests in the following areas:

i.   Current foreign policy priorities, which include:
  • Accession to the EU, of which Lilliput is a recent member;
  • Peaceful resolution of the growing unrest in Brobdignag (a neighbouring country to both Ruritania and Lilliput); and
  • A solution to the problem of Ruritanian citizens serving long jail sentences in Lilliput;
ii.   Trade and inward investment; and
iii.   Common concerns in the wider world (in particular, terrorism, drugs, human rights and the environment).

Provisional plans for the two-day visit have already been discussed and agreed with the Lilliput foreign ministry. They include:

i.   Talks and lunch with the Lilliput Foreign Minister;
ii.   Talks with the Minister for Trade and Industry;
iii.   A call on the Lilliput Prime Minister;
iv.   A speech at the Ruritanian Chamber of Commerce on the theme of why Ruritania belongs in the EU [about which Lilliput public opinion is divided];
v.   A visit to a Ruritanian company established in Lilliput and to a Lilliput company with plans for overseas expansion;
vi.   A reception for members of the Ruritanian community;
vii.   A dinner to be hosted by the Ambassador, with guests drawn from all walks of Lilliput society.

You have been tasked with constructing the media plan for the visit. How would you go about this?

11.2 Strategy

Your strategy for the media plan needs to be fully aligned with the general strategy for the visit (which should, in turn, be in line with Ruritania's overall foreign policy strategy). Your foreign minister has specified the interests he wishes to promote. The outline of the visit plan – in the preparation of which, if your embassy is sensibly organised, you will have been involved – demonstrates the means by which the visit is designed to achieve his wishes. Your own strategy should dovetail with these arrangements. You should therefore aim for media coverage, which will help to emphasise:

i.   The closeness and warmth of the bilateral relationship;
ii.   The fitness of Ruritania for EU membership;
iii.   The strength of the bilateral trading relationship and the excellent investment conditions in Ruritania;
iv.   Ruritania's responsible attitude towards the major regional and global issues.

For your strategy to be successful, you will need to have specific objectives and a clear understanding of your target audience before you can decide on the optimum means to employ.

11.3 Objectives

Under the four broad strategic aims listed above, you might have specific objectives as follows (you may well be able to think of others):

i.   Bilateral relationship
       • Achieve joint statements during the visit;
       • Get into the media a number of strong examples of recent bilateral collaboration to reinforce the immediate news following the visit;

ii.   EU membership
       • Ensure coverage of progress in political and economic reforms in Ruritania;
       • Maximise media presence at the Chamber of Commerce speech;

iii.   Trade and investment
       • Get into the media positive data about the Ruritanian economy;
       • Highlight the favourable investment conditions, with recent examples of successful inward investment;

iv.   Regional and global issues*
       • Highlight Ruritania's strong and principled stand over human rights in Brobdignag;
       • Ensure Ruritania's position on a range of global issues is understood.

       *In line with the first strategic aim, you should try to arrange joint statements on these issues whenever possible.

11.4 Target audience

For a multi-faceted visit such as this, there will be more than one target audience: this has an impact on the choice of media to be employed. The message about the strength of the bilateral relationship is aimed principally at Lilliput public opinion, so domestic news outlets, including the popular press, are therefore of greatest relevance. This is also true to a certain extent of Ruritania's desire for EU membership, although there is in addition another audience: the public in other EU countries. The trade and investment promotion is aimed at companies rather than the general public, suggesting the use of more specialised media outlets. And, finally, Ruritania's position on regional and global issues, while relevant to Lilliput, is clearly a matter of wider interest, requiring attention from the international media. It is also important not to forget the domestic media in Ruritania. Your minister will want to look good to the Ruritanian public and will be hoping for positive coverage at home to this end. Indeed, he may well be bringing the Ruritanian press corps with him. There is sometimes slight tension between the domestic political priorities of ministers – who need to be seen to be vigorously defending the national interest – and the embassy's aspirations for optimal local coverage emphasising the collaborative nature of the relationship. Managing this tension itself calls for diplomacy in its wider sense.

11.5 Media analysis

Given that there will be different audiences for different dimensions of the visit, it is essential to have a detailed catalogue of the various media outlets at your disposal: this should be an automatic reference document for any Embassy press section. The catalogue should cover newspapers, magazines, radio and television. The kind of information required is ownership, political affiliation, known prejudices (including attitudes towards Ruritania), circulation or viewing figures, and readership profile. It is worth having this analysis both for the Lilliput media and for international media (such as CNN, the Financial Times or the Wall Street Journal). The latter will undoubtedly be watched or read by certain sections of Lilliput society as well as by your international audience.

11.6 The plan

Once you have established your strategy, set objectives, identified your audiences and analysed the media at your disposal, you can prepare your plan. This is best divided into three parts: before, during and after the visit.

1. Before the visit

The minimal requirement in advance of the visit is a press release containing a formal announcement. This needs to be coordinated with the host government in order to ensure that both sides are content with the text and timing of the announcement.

The wording of the announcement might be on the following lines:

"RURITANIA FOREIGN MINISTER TO VISIT LILLIPUT

0600 Local Time, 1 April 2015 Lilliput City

Dr John Smith, Foreign Minister of the Republic of Ruritania, will be paying an official visit to Lilliput from 2 to 3 April.

This will be Dr Smith's first visit to Lilliput as foreign minister. He will hold talks with his opposite number, Madam Sara García, and will meet other members of the Lilliput Government, visit local companies and meet representatives of the Ruritanian community. Dr Smith will also make a speech at the Ruritanian Chamber of Commerce about Ruritania's candidacy for membership of the European Union.

The talks with the Lilliput Government will cover collaboration in trade and investment, security and other regional and global issues of joint concern. There will also be discussion of a possible prisoner exchange agreement.

Dr Smith trained as a surgeon and has been a member of parliament since 2001. He previously held the post of Health Minister. Dr Smith is married with two daughters."

[Appended to the press release would be background information on Ruritania- Lilliput relations, including e.g. trade and investment statistics and a list of recent ministerial visits between the two countries plus a detailed biographical note on Dr Smith.]

The press release should also appear on your own Foreign Ministry website.

A further possibility would be an article placed in a leading local newspaper on the eve of the visit, perhaps signed by the minister, or even – if circumstances permitted – by both the minister and his host. The advantage of a joint article would be to demonstrate to the public the closeness of the relationship. The downside is that you might need to dilute some of the messages you wished to convey if the text had to be agreed by both sides.

The content of such an article needs to be judged with care. It is a trailer for the main event, so you do not wish to use too much of the material that will be deployed in, for example, the Chamber of Commerce speech. Broad themes are best, with an emphasis on the positive nature of the relationship and plans for continued collaboration.

A variation on the above theme would be an exclusive interview with the minister to be published in a local newspaper. From your point of view, the best way of organising this – if the newspaper concerned agreed – would be to have written questions to which your foreign ministry, in consultation with the embassy, would provide written answers.

Another device for drawing attention to the visit would be to prepare a country supplement, financed by advertising from companies trading between the two countries, to be published in a leading newspaper on the first day of the visit. The advantage of such a supplement is that it guarantees publication of all the information you wish to get across about Ruritania. It cannot, however, guarantee that the information will actually be read: such supplements inevitably meet a degree of reader resistance.

You might also want to consider gathering together selected journalists, about a week in advance, to talk about the visit and sensitize them to the main issues surrounding it. As press officer you should be working full-time to be on good terms with key journalists: this would be a natural continuation of your regular cultivation of them.

Just before the visit itself, you should assemble press kits for distribution to journalists at different points during the visit. The core of these should be an outline programme of the visit and full biographical details, with a photograph, of the Minister. There should also be factual information, with statistics, about Ruritania and Ruritania-Lilliput relations (with recent examples of significant collaboration), together with an account of Ruritania's political and economic reforms, its EU aspirations and its general position on the global issues expected to be discussed. As the visit progresses, you can add to the kit such items as the joint statement you hope will emerge from the government discussions and the text – embargoed if necessary – of the Chamber of Commerce speech.

Finally, you should clear in advance everything you are planning with the Minister's own press officials: there should be no surprises once he arrives. Arrangements for the visit in its totality will, of course, have been cleared with the Minister's staff, but this should not preclude you from touching base with the relevant officials over media coverage.

2. During the visit

It is important to be realistic about the extent of media coverage you can, or should, expect to achieve. There are several factors that can affect this. The first is the relative importance of Ruritania, which is only a middle-ranking power: your Minister's visit will not get the same coverage as a visit by the US Secretary of State or the Chinese Foreign Minister. The second is what else is currently in the news: another Arab Spring or a nuclear meltdown somewhere could well eclipse the visit. Then there is the Minister himself. Does he like dealing with the media? Is he good at it? Will his programme allow time for all the things you would like him to do or will he insist on down time rather than meeting yet more journalists? These types of questions need to be addressed with the Minister's staff well in advance.

Assuming that the Minister is not totally media-phobic, you will wish to focus on three principal events: the government talks; the Chamber of Commerce speech; and the trade and investment-related visits.

a) Government talks

The best device for generating publicity for the government talks is a press conference immediately after the event. Given that your aim is to emphasise the closeness of the bilateral relationship, this should ideally – on this occasion – be a combined event. The standard format is to have a joint statement summarising the subjects discussed and, where relevant, agreements reached. This would be followed by whatever the two ministers might want to add individually, and then by a question-and-answer session. For the sake of speed, the statement will largely – though not entirely – have been drafted in advance on the basis of pre-negotiation between officials from both sides. It will require amendment/additions to take into account, for example, an agreement on prisoner exchange or the latest developments in Brobdignag.

You will want an extensive media presence at the press conference, which will be broad in its content. This means that you will have to work closely with the Lilliput Foreign Ministry to ensure that all the journalists relevant to you, from the local, international and Ruritanian media, receive invitations.

After the press conference, your Minister will be available for one-to-one interviews with television and radio stations. These should have been agreed in advance with stations selected to give optimal coverage to the Minister's key messages, including internationally and back in Ruritania. Make sure you warn the Minister before the interview if there is anything in particular he needs to know about the interviewer or the station concerned.

b) Chamber of Commerce Speech

The theme of the Chamber of Commerce speech is Ruritania's candidacy for EU membership. In addition to the Chamber's members, who are mainly business people, those attending on the day will be invited guests, many of them from the Lilliput Government. All of these will be likely to regard the prospect of Ruritania's EU membership with approval.

The real audience for the speech, therefore, are the people of Lilliput, many of whom are opposed to Ruritanian membership. This means that it is important to ensure that the media presence at the speech goes wider than the local financial and business press, and beyond the quality dailies, to include the popular press. Bear in mind also the public in other EU countries and remember the international media. If the Minister is up for it, you might consider an exclusive one-on-one interview with a popular television or radio station, or with a popular newspaper, after he has delivered his speech.

c) Trade and investment-related visits

The Minister is visiting two companies: a Ruritania company that has invested in Lilliput, and a Lilliput company you hope may be persuaded to invest in Ruritania. Such visits provide excellent photo opportunities – always assuming the companies concerned are producing something reasonably photogenic. Your audience on this particular occasion is largely the business community, suggesting a focus on the more specialised press, possibly to include an exclusive interview with the leading business paper.

3. After the visit

Visits are rapidly forgotten by the media and the public, but at least today the technology exists to keep the messages of the visit alive. An edited video of the press conference and a video and text of the Chamber of Commerce speech can, for example, go on the embassy and Ruritania website, and can also be mailed to a wider range of media and other contacts.

You will also want to send details of the media coverage obtained to the Minister's office as part of the overall assessment of the success or otherwise of the visit. Enumerating column inches or television and radio minutes is the most rough and ready way of measuring immediate success. Determining the impact on attitudes is considerably more difficult, as we shall see when we come to look at public diplomacy campaigns in Chapter 13.

11.7 Conclusions

There are many devices that can be used to generate media coverage. These have been examined in Chapter 9, while the current chapter offers suggestions as to how they might be applied in practice. Irrespective of the techniques deployed, the success of a media plan rests on the principles that are repeated throughout this book: know your message, know your audience and prepare with care.

Chapter 12

How to be Interviewed

United Nations Secretary-General Interviewed by radio station
UN Photo/Mark Garten

12.1 Introduction

Being interviewed on television or radio is a common experience for diplomats, whether or not they are specialised in public diplomacy. Many of the principles involved in speech-making (see Chapter 8) are relevant to being interviewed. However, there are also major differences deriving from the relative lack of control the interviewee has over the process and from the peculiarities of television in particular. In this lesson, we shall explore the means of achieving a successful interview.

12.2 Spontaneous or arranged?

If an interview is arranged, the interviewee has time to prepare. Much of this lesson is concerned with preparation, without which the interview is unlikely to be successful.

But what if there is no time for preparation? What if you are "door-stepped" as you emerge from your embassy on your way to deal with an unexpected crisis? You have to say something – and it cannot simply be "no comment", which is like a red rag to a bull to the media and can give rise to negative headlines such as "embassy officials declined to comment etc". If you are dealing with a consular emergency such as a plane crash, or with a local coup d'Etat, this will make you sound heartless and unengaged.

The answer, of course, is that you should not set foot outside the embassy door without first having prepared some brief form of words to express concern or regret as appropriate and offer some factual material, even if it is only to say that at this stage the full story is unclear and that you are urgently trying to establish the true picture. You can then excuse yourself by explaining that you are dealing with an emergency and have to get on.

12.3 Hostile or friendly?

Interviews fall very broadly into two categories: friendly or hostile. If the interview is friendly you will have the opportunity to say what you want without being permanently contradicted or interrupted. If it is hostile, you are in for a far more difficult time.

In the event of a spontaneous hostile interview – in which, perhaps, your embassy is accused of not responding fast enough to a crisis – you have no choice but to make the best of a bad situation, use your prepared material if it is relevant and move on as rapidly as possible.

In the case of a request for an arranged interview that looks likely to be hostile, you do have a choice: to be interviewed or not to be interviewed. Here you have to make a judgement – what will cause the most damage to your country's interests: to run the risk of being humiliated in the interview, or to allow your arguments to go by default if you decline to appear? If you feel the danger of humiliation is too great, it is perfectly acceptable to say that you are not available and to offer a written statement of your government's position on the subject of the interview instead.

In thinking about interviews, therefore, you might envisage them as follows:

TYPE OF INTERVIEW	SPONTANEOUS	ARRANGED
HOSTILE	!	?
FRIENDLY	OK	OK

Thankfully, in real life, it is relatively rare for an interviewer to be unremittingly hostile. He/she is after all concerned to provide an interesting and informative occasion, which he/she cannot do without a degree of cooperation from you. By the same token, friendly interviews do not guarantee that you will not be asked difficult questions. Some of the best television and radio interviewers cultivate a sympathetic persona that can be very effective in lulling their interviewees into a false sense of security so that they sometimes say things they later regret.

If you are not expecting the interview to be hostile, and it turns out to be so, there are certain rules to which you should aim to adhere, as we shall see below.

12.4 Live or recorded?

Both live and recorded interviews have their advantages and perils. The advantage of a recorded interview – provided you trust the integrity of the interviewer – is that you can get a second or third chance at making a point if you fear you have made a mess of it on the first take. The disadvantage is that an unscrupulous interviewer can have the interview edited in order to make you look bad. In general, therefore, it is better for interviews that lie towards the hostile end of the spectrum to be conducted live. Even then there is no guarantee that the interview will not be shown again on later editions of news programmes, when it will invariably be edited – quite possibly only with a view to shortening it, but often with unfortunate effects. This is one of the reasons – but not the only one – why it is best to answer questions immediately, before embarking on lengthy explanations (see below).

12.5 What to do and what to avoid

1. Preparation

As with most things in life, preparation is essential for success in being interviewed.

We have seen, in Lesson 8, that the key questions to ask when writing a speech are:

i.   What message do you wish to convey?
ii.   To whom are you speaking?

These are also the most important questions to ask before being interviewed. What is the fundamental message you wish to get across in the interview? If you cannot answer that question, you have no right agreeing to be interviewed at all. Depending on the expected length of the interview, can you break your message down into three or four succinct sound-bites, each containing a point you wish to communicate to your audience? Have you got supporting material at your fingertips to illustrate your points or to respond to challenges from the interviewer? And who exactly is your audience? In one sense, it is the interviewer himself, so you need to know as much about him as you can. What are his/her beliefs and prejudices? What sort of questions is he/she likely to be asking (so that you can have defensive material ready as required)? But the real audience are the viewers and listeners, and you also need to know as much about them as you can in order to pitch your performance at the right level.

2. The Interview

The following is a list of ten things you should and should not do during the interview:

i.   You know what you want to say: make sure you say it. A skilful interviewer may draw you down avenues of his/her own choice, taking you away from your core message. Don't let this happen: insist, but courteously, on making the points you have prepared.
ii.   Don't change the policy. Some interviewers are very good at creating an atmosphere a little like a university debate, where they will seek to persuade you by reasoned arguments that your government has got things wrong. Honest dialogue is one thing, but surrendering your government's position in front of a television audience is to be avoided.
iii.   Remain calm. The interviewer may be offensive, ignorant or wilfully inaccurate – or all three. Under no circumstances should you respond in anger, because this is precisely what the interviewer is trying to achieve. An interviewee who loses his or her temper will lose the good will of the audience. They will also be unable to think clearly and may find themselves losing the argument as well. Be polite, but firm, in pointing out the errors in the interviewer's position.
iv.   Keep your hands still and avoid over-acting. The kind of gestures that work perfectly well in a public speech can appear manic on television. Facial expressions are also exaggerated by the camera. As far as physical movements are concerned, in a television interview, less is more.
v.   Don't look down. Shyness sometimes makes people with little interview experience avert their gaze when talking. This is a mistake: look the interviewer firmly in the eye.
vi.   Speak slowly and clearly.

vii. Answer the questions. There are two points here. The first is that deliberately avoiding answering a question makes the interviewee look dishonest or inexpert. The second is that some interviewees have a tendency to launch into a lengthy explanation of their answer before they actually give it. This irritates the audience, and if the interviewer interrupts to pick up on a point in the explanation, the answer may never get given. So: answer first, explain afterwards. If you simply do not know the answer to the question, and it is within the legitimate remit of the interview, you should be honest about your ignorance and offer to provide the information after the interview.

viii. It is however permissible to refuse to answer questions you have made clear in advance you are not prepared to deal with (for example, questions about the personal life of your head of government). The interviewer may try to insist, but you are within your rights to resist such attempts.

ix. Know when to stop. Some people get carried away with their answers and talk at inordinate length. An interviewer may allow such interviewees to carry on, either out of courtesy, or because they are entertainingly making fools of themselves. Make your points concise and succinct.

x. After the interview, make sure the microphone is turned off. An incautious remark at this point can ruin what might have been a perfect interview.

12.6 Conclusions

There is no point in being interviewed if you have nothing to say. Know what you want to say, say it clearly and courteously and do not allow yourself to be deflected from your message. There is no harm in being a little nervous – it is preferable to being complacent. Be prepared for the worst – but, above all, simply be prepared.

Chapter 13

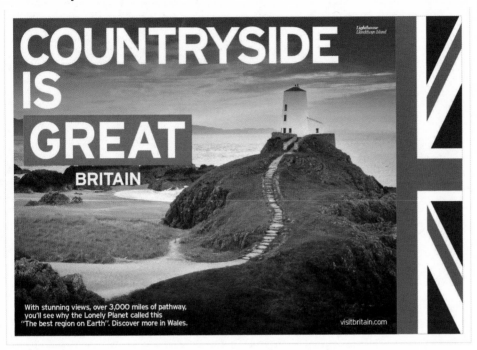

Public Diplomacy Campaigns

Example of a global advertisement campaign run by
the British government in 2011

13.1 Introduction

In Chapter 7 we examined the tools and techniques available to public diplomacy practitioners. Most of these tools and techniques are for the most part deployed on an ongoing basis in line with governments' overall policy aims (for example, many scholarship and exchange programmes have effectively become permanent). Sometimes, however, they are integrated into a campaign designed to serve a specific purpose.[150] In this chapter we shall be considering how to construct a public diplomacy campaign, drawing on what we have learned so far.

Before we do so, however, there is one important – and somewhat depressing – fact to grasp: the indispensable ingredient of a successful public diplomacy campaign is luck.

Luck is largely a matter of timing. The most brilliantly conceived and executed campaign to persuade global opinion of the benefits of expanding offshore oil exploration will fail if it happens to coincide with a massive oil spill. A drive to increase tourism to a particular country will have little success if it is followed immediately by a major volcanic eruption. Efforts to generate public support for a Middle East peace initiative may founder on a sudden outbreak of violence.

Leaving aside truly unforeseeable acts of God, there is, however, much that can be done to shorten the odds in one's favour. The key is careful preparation. We shall therefore look first at the preparations required before setting about designing a public diplomacy campaign.

13.2 Preparing for a public diplomacy campaign

A word of warning before we begin.

Every public diplomacy campaign is different: there is no definitive blueprint that will determine success. There are, however, certain questions that must be addressed before constructing a campaign if it is to have any prospect of avoiding failure. These concern strategic aims, objectives, time frame, target audience, the extent to which we are "messaging" or "listening", resources and partners. Only once we are confident we have answers to these questions, can we take final decisions about the appropriate media channels and techniques to employ and be able to proceed to the execution of the campaign. The questions to be answered are examined in a logical order below. In real life, some of these questions (such as objectives and target audiences) would be addressed simultaneously. Similarly, when bidding for resources, thought needs to have been given to choices of media channels and techniques (which are discussed in Chapter 9).

Finally, please do not expect to find here detailed recommendations for the bureaucratic structures required for a public diplomacy campaign. Every country has different systems and it is unrealistic to expect these to be changed radically. It is, however, strongly recommended that one individual be unmistakably in charge of the campaign and that he or she report periodically, at pre-determined times, to a steering committee representing all the interests involved.

---

150   Public diplomacy campaigns equate to Joseph Nye's "second dimension" of public diplomacy, which he refers to as "strategic communication" (see Module 1, Lesson 1).

13.3 Strategic aims

Every public diplomacy campaign requires a strategic aim, and it is important to be very clear about what this is before embarking on a campaign. Broadly speaking, strategic aims can be divided into three categories:

i.   A national strategic priority, such as a claim to a disputed territory, or membership of a major international organisation essential to one's country's security and economic welfare;
ii. A less exalted, more immediately realisable aim, such as an increase in inward investment or tourism, or a contested appointment to an international organisation;
iii. A "non-national" aim, for example relating to climate change.

A campaign may sometimes incorporate all three kinds of aims, but such a campaign is difficult to manage. To be successful, it would require a powerful strategic vision and a capacity for prioritising possibly clashing objectives, entailing an extremely robust co-ordinating mechanism.

13.4 Objectives

Under the overall strategic aim, it is essential to have clear, specific objectives to be achieved in pursuit of the aim, and by which to measure the success of the campaign.

The success of a campaign supporting a claim to disputed territory would, of course, be demonstrated by the actual ceding to one's country of sovereignty over the territory. In reality, however, this level of success is highly unlikely in the short term, so subordinate objectives would be necessary. These might include a measurable movement in one's country's favour in international opinion polls, or a majority vote on the subject in a relevant United Nations body. Interim success in aspirations to join a major international organisation might also be measured through movements in opinion polls.

Where the strategic aim is more confined, it becomes easier to set more precisely measurable objectives (although see here also Chapter 14). An increase in inward investment can be assessed by value, or by numbers of investment decisions. Increases in tourism can also be measured by numbers and tourism expenditure. Similarly, a candidate to, for example, a United Nations appointment will either get the job or will not.

"Non-national" aims, for example reducing global carbon emissions, call for a different kind of objective, such as positive movements in public opinion polls on the science of climate change.

13.5 Timeframe

All public diplomacy campaigns require a clear timeframe. This is necessary to allow for sensible budgeting for the required resources and to be able to judge success.

In theory, there are campaigns that have no time limit. It is not difficult to think of long-standing territorial disputes, where the positions of both sides are so deeply entrenched that nothing short of war is likely to bring a resolution. In such cases, one side or the other – and frequently both – will persist in reiterating their claim publicly at every conceivable opportunity. Such ongoing action tends, however, to be largely defensive, and to ensure that the claim is not weakened by default. An active public diplomacy campaign in support of such a claim would require a timeframe of some kind, even if it were five, or ten years, or even longer, for there to be any prospect of judging its success. A timeframe of this dimension would also be appropriate for a campaign to support, for example, entry into the European Union.

Where the campaign is in support of a more limited objective, such as increased inward investment or tourism, the timeframe will tend to be shorter, perhaps between a year and five years – and in the latter case, with interim yearly targets. A campaign for a UN appointment might last only a matter of months.

The timeframe for a campaign for "non-national" aims will vary according to the issue and circumstances. If, for example, there is an upcoming climate summit in a year's time, the strategic aim might be to achieve, by the date of the summit, an observable increase in public support in key countries for legally enforceable measures to control carbon emissions.

In summary, a well-planned campaign requires, before anything else, a clear strategic aim, supported by specific objectives, to be achieved within a specified timeframe.

13.6 Target audience

There are two questions to be asked about the target audience. Where are they? And who are they?

It is possible that the people you are seeking to influence are those living in the country next door. Or they may be your regional neighbours. Alternatively, you may be aiming at an audience beyond the region, in countries targeted for a particular reason. You may even be trying to influence people in every country in the world. Which is it? You need to know the answer to this question if you are to use the appropriate media outlet (see also Chapter 9).

Similarly, you need to be clear about the kind of people you want to reach. The types of questions you need to ask are the following. Do they form part of the political elite? Are they businessmen, bankers or from the professional classes? Are they academics? Labour leaders? Journalists? Are they running NGOs? Are they old or young? Rich or poor? Believers or non-believers? Or are you aiming at literally everyone? Only by answering these questions will you be in a position to make informed decisions about the content of your campaign and the media and tools to deploy.

13.7 "Messaging" or "Listening"?

Let us remind ourselves again of the spectrum of public diplomacy modes suggested by Ali Fisher and Aurélie Bröckerhoff:

LISTENING
Listening shows respect and it may sometimes actually change behaviour. But it must be genuine: and, on its own, it is limited in scope.

FACILITATION
Facilitation entails helping others to achieve their goals, for example Norway's efforts to advance the MEPP.

BUILDING NETWORKS or LONG-TERM RELATIONSHIPS
This is the process of identifying and cultivating people likely to be of influence in the future: it offers no immediate return.

CULTURAL EXCHANGE
This is a reciprocal activity.

CULTURAL DIPLOMACY
This is moving towards messaging, i.e. "telling a story".

BROADCASTING
By definition, broadcasting entails, above all, transmitting, although there will not necessarily be direct government messaging involved if the broadcaster enjoys editorial independence.

DIRECT MESSAGING (TELLING)
At this end of the spectrum lie nation branding, tourism promotion, policy advocacy and information correction.[151]

Where do we want to be on this spectrum in our public diplomacy campaign? Thinking about this will help us to choose the best option for the purpose we have in mind. Very importantly, it will help us identify the best potential partners.

It is important to be flexible and adopt the appropriate mode for different components of the campaign. But remember: if you spend all the time "telling", you may not gain your objectives, because your target audience may simply not "get" the message.

---

151   Ali Fisher and Aurélie Bröckerhoff, 2008.

13.8 Resources

All public diplomacy campaigns are inevitably constrained by resources. It is therefore important to have an inventory of what is available before constructing the campaign.

The obvious resource constraint will be the budget. There is a certain chicken-and-egg element to this, because you need a general idea of what you want to do in order to bid for the funds to do it. This will entail some preliminary consideration of the choice of media (see Chapter 9), but the final decisions on this cannot be taken until you know how much money you have to spend.

The budget is, however, only one of the resources available to you. You have a ready-made diplomatic network. You also have access to staff in other government departments with an interest in the strategic aim you have set yourself. You have ministers, parliamentarians and other VIPs who travel and can help spread the word. You have in-house expertise you can tap into, and external expertise you can buy (given the budget).

You also have a range of possible partners (see below).

13.9 Partners

One of the advantages for governments of the changes we have observed in the international realm (see in particular Chapter 5) is that the increased significance of non-state actors – which in itself challenges the dominance of states' activity – also offers great potential for partnerships.

According to the strategic aim – and the individual objectives within that aim –, governments can look for collaboration from companies, NGOs, universities, think tanks, trades unions, cultural institutions, diasporas and many more. With government budgets under serious strain, there are straightforward financial reasons for doing this.

However, there are other reasons as well. Non-state actors frequently offer expertise and experience that is not available to governments. They may also enhance the credibility of a campaign by virtue of the simple fact that they are distinct from governments. This may not, however, necessarily be the case if the aim of the campaign is so strongly policy-related that only governments can be expected to speak authoritatively on the subject.

Taking into account the answers to the questions you have asked yourself so far, the identities of relevant potential partners will be clear. You will need to sound them out immediately regarding their willingness to collaborate, so that you can factor this information in due course into your campaign proposals. From now on you must also keep them involved in the decision-making process.

13.10 Designing the campaign

With the strategic aim, objectives and target audience decided, with resources secured and partners identified, detailed decisions about media and techniques of communication can be made. Provisional ideas about these are necessary for the purpose of calculating the resources required. However, final decisions can only be made once those resources are secured. It is worth stressing again that every campaign is different, and that there is no overall blueprint for these decisions. The important thing is to consider all the possibilities and decide what is best for your particular campaign.

13.11 Choice of media channel

1. Traditional media outlets: press, television, radio

As we have seen when designing a media plan (Chapter 11), careful selection of media outlets is necessary to enhance the prospects of reaching our target audience. If your target audience are members of the political elite in a neighbouring country, you will select the press or television and radio programmes of that country they are likely to use, plus key international media players. If, on the other hand, you are trying to reach potential inward investors from East Asia, you will look for the media relevant to business, both in their region and internationally. Likewise, if your objective is tourism, you will aim for more popular outlets, and so on.

2. Digital technologies

It goes without saying that the campaign should feature prominently on your website, and that component events should be trailed and reported, both there and, as appropriate, via e-mail, social networks and texting. Social media will allow you to broadcast widely or target selectively as required. If your target audience is young people, these are likely to be the only media through which to reach them.

3. Personal contact

The media referred to above provide channels of communication to large numbers of people. Judicious selection of media outlets, and the even more precise targeting facilitated by digital technologies, allow communication to be established with the people we most wish to influence.

However, for optimal communication – as those who have experienced video-conferencing will know – the best medium remains personal face-to-face contact. Many of the techniques we look at below entail such contact.

13.12 Tools and techniques

Your choice of media has been determined by your objectives and target audience. These will also influence the tools and techniques you deploy, as will where you choose to be operating on the Fisher-Bröckerhoff spectrum.

At one end of the spectrum is paid advertising. This is perfectly legitimate for aims such as boosting tourism, but would appear less appropriate – although it is used by some governments – in pursuit of a political cause.

Broadcasting, for those governments exercising editorial control, comes next. Here, however, you risk straying into the realms of propaganda (Chapter 3), unless the campaign aims are not national ones. Then come the various ways of involving the media (as examined in Chapter 9): group discussions, interviews, press conferences, articles, briefings, press releases and so on. Which of these best suit your purpose? How can you most easily fit them into the campaign timetable (see below)? How can you make them happen?

Speeches deserve separate mention, because media coverage will flow from a well-timed keynote speech (remember again President Obama's 2009 speech in Cairo). Speeches, and media coverage more generally, will come with outward visits, preferably at the most senior level achievable.

High-level visits may accompany exhibitions, seminars and conferences. However, these latter also stand on their own – whether held overseas or at home – as ways of advancing the aims of a public diplomacy campaign. It does not matter whether the subject is business, politics, international conflict or global challenges: the point is that such events expose people – and their ideas – directly to each other. The very holding of these events – assuming they are successful – will redound to the credit of the organiser, as is true of cultural and sporting events.

Sponsored inward visits are an excellent way of exposing key people of influence to the ideas we wish to convey. Training and scholarships schemes are for building longer-term relationships, but the announcement of such schemes – or of important and positive changes to them – can generate helpful publicity for a public diplomacy campaign.

13.13 Timetabling

It is all well and good to know what you want to say, whom you want to influence and the means you intend employ to do so. But how do you put this all together into a persuasive package? The answer is by careful timetabling.

Like a symphony, or a well-constructed play, a successful public diplomacy programme requires structure and pacing. It is no good doing everything simultaneously, but at the same time you do not want the component parts of your campaign to seem random and unconnected.

Ideally – although this is not always achievable – you would start with a bang, have a powerful centrepiece event, a final crescendo and – very importantly – a series of linking events or activities to help publicise these high points.

The ways in which you achieve this structure will vary according to circumstances. Often it is a matter of exploiting existing opportunities. If you are working up to, say, a climate summit or a major world-sporting event, you already have the focus for your final crescendo. If, for example, your foreign minister, or head of government, or other ministers, are already scheduled to visit countries containing your target audience, or if your national orchestra is on tour in the region, you have a potential basis for either the centrepiece event or for jump-starting the campaign. Once you have the outline structure containing these high points, you can flesh out the campaign accordingly.

If you are working on the campaign in the home capital, you will inevitably devolve the detailed programming to your embassies in the countries concerned. If you are in an overseas embassy, you will be deploying your local expertise and contacts to set up events that will fit into the overarching structure of the campaign. In either case, critical path analysis will be an important element in your planning.

13.14 Evaluation

We have from time to time referred to the question of measuring the success of public diplomacy activity. We shall now consider some of the ways in which you might measure the success of your campaign.

We have already observed that the private sector, in general, is able to measure success with relative ease. Revenues, market share, profitability and, where relevant, the share price are all things on which a numerical value can be placed. It is not difficult to establish a correlation between movements in these values and the marketing activities that precede them – even if it is not always possible to demonstrate precise causation.

Because, as a rule, governments are seeking arguably less tangible outcomes, evaluation of public diplomacy campaigns can as a result be more difficult. The easy part is measuring inputs and outputs: how many visits, speeches, column inches, television minutes, website hits and so forth have been achieved. Outcomes are more difficult to judge, although the principle is simple and boils down to three questions. Where are you now? Where do you hope to be at the end of the campaign? How did you do?

In some cases, you can measure success in a similar way as the private sector. If you are promoting tourism, for example, you will have statistics about current annual tourist arrivals and how much they spend. You should also have these figures segmented into, for example, package holidaymakers (low spenders) and independent travellers (generally higher spenders), or other categories, including age, first time visitors and so on. This information will allow you to identify the target audience you most want to influence and to set objectives accordingly. The same information in a year's time, for instance, will enable you to judge how successful you have been.

Similarly, in the case of inward investment, you will have a base figure of value or units of foreign investment, or annual figures for new investment, on which you can construct numerical targets for increases, and against which your campaign can be judged. As we have observed above, you may only be able to demonstrate correlation: causation is always elusive. A strong correlation, if there is no other explanation for it, is nevertheless highly satisfying. It is also possible to fashion questionnaires to ask people on an ex post facto basis what motivated them to visit or invest, although their responses are not always totally reliable.

We are, however, in more problematic territory when it comes to campaigns with a political motivation. Here, the traditional means of measuring success are opinion polls. Some polls are published independently on a regular basis (such as the Pew Global Attitudes Project[152]). There is also, for example, the Anholt-GfK Roper Nations Brand Index (see Chapter 3) and the Institute for Government global ranking of soft power (see Chapter 2). There are also more precisely focused rankings, such as the Global Competitiveness Report of the World Economic Forum (WEF).[153] However, it is difficult to link these measures of popularity or success to a specific public diplomacy campaign as opposed to the objective achievements themselves of the countries concerned – or, at least, others' perceptions of them.

When a campaign has a clear aim, such as shifting public opinion in EU countries about another country's possible accession, it is possible to commission customised polls, focus groups or interviews to measure its success. Even in such cases, it is difficult to disentangle the impact of the campaign itself from that of the genuine political and economic reforms the country concerned may be introducing.
For a more detailed discussion of the importance – and difficulty – of public diplomacy evaluation more generally, see Chapter 14.

13.15 Risk assessment

We observed at the beginning of this chapter that the indispensable element to a successful public diplomacy campaign is luck, and that luck is largely a question of timing. It is therefore important to ask yourself the question before you embark upon detailed planning: could this be the wrong time for a campaign? The answer is clearly yes if events in the real world have conspired against you as in the examples given at the beginning of this chapter. However, there may be other contemporaneous developments that, while not directly linked, would distract attention from the campaign. Whatever the subject of the campaign, it would need to go on hold at the time of, for example, a catastrophic natural disaster such as a tsunami or a terrorist attack of the dimension of 9/11.

There are other questions you need to ask. Might the campaign be misunderstood? Might you be dismissed as propagandists? If so, would the damage we caused be greater than that from inaction? There are no easy answers to these questions, no metrics to assist in the calculation. It comes down in the end to judgement in each individual case.

13.16 Past successes and failures

While every campaign is different, it can be instructive to look at past campaigns that have either succeeded or failed. Nicholas Cull of the University of Southern California has assembled a set of case studies demonstrating successes and failures under five headings: listening, advocacy, cultural diplomacy,

152   Pews Global Attitude Project: http://www.pewglobal.org/   (Retrieved August 2015).
153   http://www.weforum.org/issues/global-competitiveness   (Retrieved August 2015).

exchange and international broadcasting. The successes variously feature, inter alia, sound policies (above all), listening research, limited objectives, careful audience selection, well-crafted youth exchanges and advocacy by third parties. In the failures, the most common mistaken assumption is that appearance and reality can somehow be two different things without the audience ever noticing.[154]

13.17 Conclusions

In this chapter we have discussed a series of questions that need to be asked when preparing a public diplomacy campaign. When – and only when - we have satisfactory answers to these questions, we can go ahead and construct our detailed campaign plan.

Remember, finally, that no public diplomacy campaign can perform miracles: it will not have any positive influence if it does not accord with your government's actual policies or the facts on the ground. No one will be persuaded of your benign intentions if you go to war. No one will invest in your country if you have tiresome bureaucratic restrictions. In addition, very few will be persuaded to return as tourists if they are subjected to delay and discourtesy by immigration officials. Getting things right in the first place is the only sound basis for public diplomacy to succeed.

154   Nicholas J. Cull, *Public Diplomacy: Lessons from the Past*, CDC Perspectives on Public Diplomacy, US Center on Public Diplomacy at the Annenberg School, University of Southern California, 2009: http://uscpublicdiplomacy.org/publications/perspectives/CPDPerspectivesLessons.pdf (Retrieved August 2015). In addition to the ten case studies, Cull offers a helpful survey of public diplomacy past, present and future.

Chapter 14

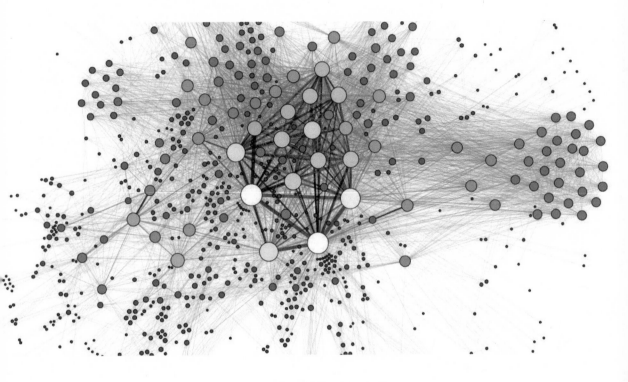

Evaluation

14.1 Introduction

We have already observed the importance of having clear, measurable objectives, but also some of the obvious difficulties in judging the success of public diplomacy activity. Efforts to develop meaningful evaluation of public diplomacy have increased considerably in the period since 9/11. In this chapter we shall be looking at evaluation in more detail.

Much of what follows is drawn from valuable work carried out in 2011 by Robert Banks, a former United States public diplomacy practitioner, who has constructed a resource guide to public diplomacy evaluation published by the University of Southern California.[155] While emphasising the point that public diplomacy evaluation is complex, crosses disciplinary boundaries and is susceptible to many different approaches, Banks nevertheless offers some general conclusions based on his personal experience and the extensive bibliography he has compiled.

14.2 Challenges

Banks identifies what he describes as "The Dirty Dozen" problems afflicting public diplomacy evaluation. These are:

i. Impact can often be seen only over the long term;
ii. Public diplomacy evaluation measures concepts that are intangible;
iii. Results may not be directly attributable to public diplomacy intervention;
iv. Tracking elites is often not sustainable over time;
v. Evaluation is time-, labour- and cost-intensive;
vi. Because professional evaluation is relatively new, baseline data often do not exist;
vii. Changes in political leadership at home and in public diplomacy staff in the field can affect the continuity of evaluation regimes;
viii. The growing emphasis on multilateral, inter-agency, coalition and public-private partnership approaches to addressing global issues can complicate evaluation strategies;
ix. The proliferation of new media technologies requires new approaches to evaluation;
x. Institutions, governments included, prefer success stories;
xi. There is often confusion about the difference between output and outcomes;
xii. Public diplomacy has attracted limited academic attention.

This list includes formidable difficulties, with which even the most powerful and well-resourced governments are grappling with variable results.[156]

---

155   Robert Banks, *A Resource Guide to Public Diplomacy Evaluation*, Figueroa Press Los Angeles, November 2011 (CPD Perspectives, USC Centre on Public Diplomacy at the Annenberg School, University of Southern California). http://uscpublicdiplomacy.org/publications/perspectives/CPD_Perspectives_Paper%209_2011.pdf (Retrieved August 2015).
What Banks has to say is informed by considerable professional experience. He has also assembled a formidable bibliography of great value to any student wishing to study evaluation in greater depth.
156   For an illustration of how difficult the United States Government finds evaluating its public diplomacy activities, see *US Public Diplomacy: Key issues for Congressional Oversight*, US Government Accountability Office Report to Congressional Committees, May 2009: http://books.google.co.uk/books?id=hSYdWZlJcwQC&pg=PA18&lpg=PA18&dq=public+diplomacy+indicators&source=bl&ots=uYVi8p2PlN&sig=IMM2uC9vXGsoP5U50k716qrdPdw&hl=en&sa=X&ei=FzS2T8v7Flj80QWcj8igCg&ved=0CFoQ6AEwBg#v=onepage&q=public%20diplomacy%20indicators&f=false (Retrieved August 2015).

14.3 Benefits

Alongside this discouraging list of challenges, Banks still emphasises the benefits of a strong evaluation regime:

i.   Evaluation can lead to better allocation of resources;
ii.   It can help organisations justify budget requests;
iii.   Evaluation can reveal public diplomacy best practice;
iv.   It can motivate staff to improve performance;
v.   Evaluation can moderate inflated expectations of what public diplomacy can reasonably be expected to achieve;[157]
vi.   If public diplomacy can be shown to produce concrete results, it can provide an alternative to hard power;
vii.   Performance measurement can help build a domestic constituency for public diplomacy;
viii. Demonstrating effectiveness through evaluation can give public diplomacy a seat at the policymaker's table;
ix.   Evaluation forces the public diplomacy practitioner to confront assumptions and answer the "so what" question.

Despite the difficulties involved, therefore, there are powerful incentives to try to measure the success of public diplomacy activity.

14.4 How to administer evaluation

Banks identifies the following common factors in successful evaluation regimes:

i.   Leadership buy-in (to avoid simple box-checking by public diplomacy staff);
ii.   A systematic approach (i.e., evaluation should be built into the organisational framework, not an add-on);
iii.   A strategic plan for evaluation;
iv.   Independent evaluations;
v.   Clear, measurable objectives connected to the organisational mission[158];
vi.   Training of public diplomacy staff in evaluation methods;
vii.   Actionable data (if there is no use for the information, there is no point in collecting it);
viii. Stakeholder involvement;
ix.   Adequate resource allocation;[159]

---

157   Banks urges further research into public diplomacy's sphere of influence, making clear that in his view it cannot "move the needle" at the macro level, but is able to do so as its focus is reduced. He also advocates personal contact (Edward R Murrow's "the last three feet"), observing that, ironically, the trend is in the opposite direction, with increasing use of digital technologies (Robert Banks, 2011).

158   Logic models allow for the tracing of a course from high-level goals, through long-term outcomes, intermediate outcomes, outputs and activities, and finally to inputs. For an excellent account of a pilot project based on this approach run jointly by the Foreign and Commonwealth Office (FCO). and the British Council, see: Louise Vintner and David Knox. "*Measuring the Impact of Public Diplomacy: Can It Be Done?*" in Engagement: Public Diplomacy in a Globalized World. Foreign and Commonwealth Office, July 2008. (Unfortunately, this excellent study is no longer readily available online.)

159   The expert advice is that 8-10% of a programme budget should be allocated to evaluation. This is, however, rarely achieved, the natural instinct of the practitioner being to maximise spend on the substance of the programme (Robert Banks, 2011).

x.   Audience research (ideally at every stage of programme implementation, although few governments have the resources for this);

xi.   "Talking the walk" (i.e. public diplomacy evaluation units proclaiming their activities more loudly);

xii.   Declassification of evaluation results;

xiii.   Embedding of public diplomacy staff in contact evaluation teams (so that they may acquire relevant expertise);

xiv.   Evaluation of the evaluators;

xv.   Incentives for public diplomacy staff to participate in evaluation (otherwise it is afforded a low priority).

14.5 What to evaluate

Historically, most public diplomacy evaluation has focused on individual programmes, such as – and most typically – exchanges or scholarships. The reasons for this are that:

i.   There is abundant historical data for comparative purposes;

ii.   As discrete entities, programmes are easier and cheaper to analyse; and

iii.   Funds are frequently earmarked for particular programmes, which generate an obligation to account for how they are spent.

The drawback to evaluating individual programmes alone is the loss of the possible efficiency benefits of comparative analysis. Cross-cutting exercises, involving clusters of programmes, are more difficult to conduct, but can be very revealing. In assessing the success of a public diplomacy campaign, which would be likely to incorporate a range of programme activity, there would be little alternative to such an approach.

A further alternative is the systems approach, which looks at all public diplomacy activities as a single "programme". This was adopted by the Bush administration in its Programme Assessment Rating Tool (PART), but discontinued under President Obama. Still under way is the Public Diplomacy Impact (PDI) initiative, launched in 2006 by the State Department's Evaluation and Measurement Unit (EMU), which seeks to measure aggregate impact by comparing the attitude of foreign elites who have participated in United States public diplomacy programmes with those who have not.[160] In September 2014, the US Advisory Commission on Public Diplomacy published a detailed report, based on a six-month enquiry, into efforts by the State Department to assess the impact of its public diplomacy activities through research, analytics, and evaluation.[161]

---

160   The survey employed by EMU in the impact assessment asks questions about: understanding of United States society, values and policies; favourability towards the United States; attitudes towards United States policies and influence globally; satisfaction with the public diplomacy programme; and receptivity to future engagement. *(Ibid)* For a description of the full range of EMU's evaluation activities, see their website: http://www.state.gov/r/ppr/emu/ (Retrieved August 2015).

161   Data Driven Public Diplomacy: Progress Towards Measuring the Impact of Public Diplomacy and International Broadcasting Activities, US Advisory Commission on Public Diplomacy, 16 September 2014: http://www.state.gov/pdcommission/reports/231733.htm (Retrieved August 2015).

Other possible approaches include frame-based assessment, i.e. focusing on cues or arguments emphasising individual aspects of a particular policy[162]; and network analysis, i.e. the examination of the structure of relationships between social entities.[163]

14.6 How to evaluate

The two basic approaches to evaluation are to analyse the process (e.g. how efficiently a programme is working) or the impact (i.e. what the actual results are). Many organisations still rely quite heavily on the first of these, for example using questionnaires at a conference to measure audience reaction to a speaker and his materials. It is far more difficult and time-consuming to construct an evaluation to determine impact: it may well require assessments not just after, but also before and during, the programme, and it involves much more analysis.

Another choice is between quantitative and qualitative analysis. The former tends to cost less, is less time-consuming and is easily read and absorbed by stakeholders and funders. The latter, involving activities such as focus groups and face-to-face interviews – and the need to observe and narrate a story – entail considerable investment in staff, money and time. In practice, the best results will come from a judicious combination of both quantitative and qualitative analysis.[164]

A further distinction is that between measuring outputs and outcomes. This is well illustrated by Banks with the example of a campaign to enhance a country's legal system. Twenty judges trained would be a satisfactory output. However, the required outcome might be successful implementation of a trial-by-jury system.[165]

The final distinction – which is related to the issue of outputs and outcomes – is between intermediate and long-term evaluation. Banks offers here a further helpful illustration involving a programme seeking to reduce trafficking of women and girls. This might begin, in the short term, with an intensive media outreach campaign to raise public awareness, followed by medium-term actions to support legislation on the subject and exchanges, conferences and so on. The long-term measures of success would be evidence of increased data-sharing between law enforcement agencies, more prosecutions and so on; and ultimately a clear reduction in trafficking. But the long term would amount to several years or more.

---

162   See Michael Egner, *Between Slogans and Solutions: A Frame-Based Assessment Methodology for Public Diplomacy*, The Pardee RAND Graduate School, 2009. See: http://www.rand.org/content/dam/rand/pubs/rgs_dissertations/2010/RAND_RGSD255.pdf and http://uscpublicdi-plomacy.org/publications/perspectives/CPDPerspectivesLessons.pdf (Retrieved August 2015). Egner argues that framing allows policy-makers to target and adjust key messages more effectively.
163   See Ali Fisher, *Mapping the Great Beyond: Identifying Meaningful Networks in Public Diplomacy*, CDC Perspectives on Public Diplomacy, US Center on Public Diplomacy at the Annenberg School, University of Southern California, April 2010: http://uscpublicdiplomacy.org/sites/uscpub-licdiplomacy.org/files/legacy/publications/perspectives/CPDPerspectivesMappingNetworks.pdf (Retrieved August 2015). Fisher advocates network analysis to determine, for example, if a public diplomacy initiative has helped to generate desired links between individual bloggers.
164   An example of this approach is to be found in the 2010/2011 British Council annual report, which combines a numerical scorecard with a narrative evaluation. See: http://www.britishcouncil.org/new/PageFiles/13001/2010-11%20AnnualReport.pdf (Retrieved August 2015).
165   Robert Banks, 2011.

Funders are often looking for quick results and – as noted above – continuity is a problem. This has led to a premium being placed on intermediate results as a "proxy" or "signal" of the long-term outcome.[166, 167]

14.7 Polling

Polling has a long history in public diplomacy evaluation and remains one of the main techniques employed. We have already referred (in Chapter 13) to examples such as the Pew Global Attitudes Project, the Anholt-GfK Roper Nations Brand Index and the Institute for Government global ranking of soft power. The problem with such generic polls from the point of view of public diplomacy evaluation is that they are too general, and there are too many external factors at work, to judge the impact public diplomacy itself is having on the results. The value of polling thus varies proportionately to its specificity. Precise polling entails the use of focus groups and interviews and is, inevitably, more expensive.

14.8 The impact of digital technologies on evaluation

As we have already seen (in Chapters 5 and 10), digital technologies have had a profound impact on the environment in which governments operate and are influencing the manner in which they practise public diplomacy. What is the contribution of digital technologies to evaluation?

One answer is that they have revolutionised it. Use of computers allows for the high-speed collation and analysis of vast amounts of data, which previously would have entailed long and painstaking human effort or have been regarded as impossible. Construction of complex public diplomacy strategies with embedded evaluation measures is made feasible by such powerful computing capacity. Ease of manipulation of statistical data has enormously facilitated measurement of the efficiency and effectiveness of public diplomacy activities.

There is a possible downside to the ease and economy with which such data can be handled, namely that it encourages quantitative analysis over necessarily more expensive and laborious qualitative analysis.

166   *Ibid.*
167   A rationale for interpreting intermediate outcomes as signposts on the journey from the short to the long term is to be found in the article referred to in footnote 158 above describing the FCO/British Council pilot project. At the level of input, resources are measured in terms of staff time and direct project spend. At the level of activity or outputs, the focus is on a systematic approach to monitoring media coverage, to the collection of feedback from participants in public diplomacy activities and to follow-up evaluation after completion of each such activity. The emphasis is at all times on evidence-based evaluation rather than narrative reporting. At the level of intermediate outcomes, impact is measured using a combination of three evaluation tools or 'trackers':
a) a media tracker which seeks to identify changes in the nature and tone of coverage of targeted   issues, and, where possible, the reasons for these changes;
b) an influencer tracker to generate information on opinion change among those individuals considered key 'influencers' on policy issues related to the intermediate outcomes. This involves systematic mapping of influencers and semi-structured interviews, repeating the process year on year in order to track changes in opinion;
c) a concrete changes tracker for recording objectively verifiable changes in the environment that are related to the intermediate outcomes, whether positive or negative.
While the evaluation framework offers valuable insights, the authors state that, given its expense, it is not intended as a tool to be employed comprehensively across the network. (Vintner and Knox, 2008).

On the other hand, through social networks it is already becoming possible as well to track qualitative achievements such as positive commentary and probable levels of influence.[168] As the software becomes more sophisticated, the scope for this kind of evaluation will grow.[169]

14.9 Conclusions

Evaluation of public diplomacy activity is difficult – and expensive – but necessary. Great strides have been made in recent years, aided by technological advances, in developing logic-driven public diplomacy strategies with provision built in for evaluation. Measuring inputs and outputs is reasonably easily achieved, and progress has been made in measuring intermediate outcomes. Confident measurement of long-term outcomes remains the Holy Grail for which all public diplomacy practitioners still strive.

---

168   The potential for this is strongly argued by Brian D. Fung, *Klout and the Evolution of Digital Diplomacy*, The Washington Post, 22 August 2011: http://www.washingtonpost.com/national/on-innovations/how-klout-could-change-americas-image-abroad/2011/08/22/glQAsoONWJ_story.html (Retrieved August 2105). See also the Klout website: http://klout.com/home (Retrieved August 2105).
169   Nicholas Cull, among others, has called for more effort from governments in this field, arguing that the systematic integration of foreign public opinion research into public diplomacy remains the most important task in the digital era, being – in his view - as neglected a field as it was in the previous epoch of public diplomacy. See: Nicholas J. Cull, *Public Diplomacy: Lessons from the Past*, CDC Perspectives on Public Diplomacy, US Center on Public Diplomacy at the Annenberg School, University of Southern California, 2009: http://uscpublicdiplomacy.org/publications/perspectives/CPDPerspectivesLessons.pdf (Retrieved August 2105).

PART 3
CONCLUSIONS

Chapter 15

Key Lessons for Public Diplomacy Practitioners

United Nations Secretary-General Ban Ki-moon visiting an international school
UN Photo/Eskinder Debebe

15.1 Public Diplomacy: What it is

Let us begin this chapter about key lessons for public diplomacy practitioners by reviewing what we have covered so far.

In Part 1 of this book we looked (in Chapter 1) at the origin in the 1960s of the expression "public diplomacy", and considered how its practice differed from that of traditional diplomacy. We observed that its essential component, seeking to influence foreign publics, long pre-dated the existence of the phrase itself. Communications theory offered the central insight that listening is the key to effective communication and we considered a spectrum of public diplomacy modes ranging from "listening" at one end to "telling" at the other. We saw that public diplomacy has three dimensions: daily communication; campaigns (described by Joseph Nye as "strategic communication"); and the development of lasting relationships.

Public diplomacy today is largely informed by Joseph Nye's concept of "soft power", i.e. getting others to want the outcomes you want by co-opting them rather than coercing them. We saw (in Chapter 2) that, while Nye is an advocate of a strong defence capability, he counsels against exclusive dependence on hard power in an age when public opinion is increasingly important in influencing government policies.

We looked (in Chapter 3) at a range of activities related to public diplomacy: nation branding, propaganda, cultural relations, public relations and lobbying. Some of these activities (nation-branding, propaganda and cultural relations) overlap with public diplomacy – some would even argue that they are integral to public diplomacy – while others, though clearly distinct (public relations and lobbying), employ principles and techniques relevant to public diplomacy. All involve knowing your message and your audience.

In tracing the development of public diplomacy (in Chapter 4), we observed that, while its origins lie a long way back in history, it was given powerful impetus by dramatic improvements in communications in the nineteenth and twentieth centuries and the increasing importance of the press and public opinion. There was a tendency for investment in public diplomacy made in times of crisis to slacken off when the crisis had passed. This happened, for example, at the end of the Second World War and of the Cold War. 9/11 once more obliged governments to focus on the subject, a process encouraged recently by budgetary constraints on military expenditure.

We discussed (in Chapter 5) the complex and ever-changing environment in which public diplomacy is practised in the 21st Century. The ICT revolution has deprived governments of their near monopoly over the control of information: through the internet, 24-hour television and mobile telephony, information is available instantly to vast numbers of people around the globe. The ubiquity of the media renders the making and execution of policy in total secrecy impossible. The growth of democracy means that governments are increasingly answerable to their populations. The blurring of the distinction between domestic and foreign policy has created an equivalent blurring between public diplomacy and "domestic socialisation" (explaining policies to one's own public). And there are increasing numbers of non-state actors, ranging from the most benign of non-governmental organisations (NGOs) to terrorist groups like Al Qaeda, disseminating their messages cost-effectively through readily accessible international networks. Such phenomena have rendered old models of public diplomacy, involving the one-way transmission of information, increasingly problematic.

Finally (in Chapter 6) we examined the legal framework for public diplomacy and suggested that there is a lacuna on this subject in public international law. Diplomatic practice stems from state sovereignty – the current articulation of which is the United Nations Charter – and has developed over time in response to wider changes in international society. Article 3 of the Vienna Convention allows states to exercise considerable discretion in public diplomacy activity – subject to the provisions of Article 41, which require respect for a receiving state's laws and regulations and non-interference in its internal affairs. This discretion is regulated – to the extent it is regulated at all – by reciprocity and mutual advantage.

15.2 Public Diplomacy: How to do it

In Part 2, we turned from the conceptual study of public diplomacy to the tools and techniques employed in its practice. Bearing in mind the "listening"/"telling" spectrum, we examined (in Chapter 7) the traditional tools of public diplomacy: cultural and educational exchange, training, seminars and conferences, exhibitions, missions, sponsored visits, broadcasting, speeches, and managing relations with the media. We considered (in Chapter 10) the impact of digital technologies and the role of websites, social networks and mobile telephony, concluding that the performance of governments seeking to grapple with the challenges presented by these technologies is variable.

Most diplomats find themselves making – or drafting – speeches. We therefore spent some time (in Chapter 8) considering the essential principles of a successful speech: knowing your message and your audience, giving your speech a clear structure, including a powerful opening and conclusion, and speaking clearly and slowly, with good eye contact and personal engagement. We emphasised the importance of preparation and rehearsal.

Despite the rapid growth of new media, the traditional media remain an essential component of creating and implementing foreign policy. In discussion of dealing with the media (in Chapter 9) we looked at the range of techniques available: press releases, statements, briefings, signed articles, speeches, press conferences, interviews, group discussions, hospitality, and press lines. We gave particular consideration to crisis management, where the paramount need is to provide the media with an immediate and credible story while ensuring that all parts of the organisation speak with the same voice.

Media coverage of crisis occurs spontaneously. For an organised event it needs to be generated. We therefore looked (in Chapter 11) at how to construct a media plan, taking the example of an overseas visit by a foreign minister. The strategic aims of the plan needed to be fully in line with the country's overall foreign policy strategy and contain measurable objectives serving those aims. The target audience had to be clearly identified and an analysis made of available media channels to ensure that they matched the chosen audience. The visit would be trailed by a press release and possibly a signed article in a local newspaper and other press briefing. During the visit itself, suitable opportunities were identified for a press conference, a speech and one-to-one interviews. After the visit, transcripts and video coverage would be posted on the embassy and foreign ministry website and e-mailed to a range of media and other contacts.

In Chapter 12, we looked at how to be interviewed on television or radio. Some of the principles of speech-making apply (notably in the preparation), but there are important differences, mainly because the interviewee has less control over events. There remains the option of declining an interview expected to be hostile if this seems to be the least damaging course of action. It is essential to be clear about the message you wish to convey and to know the audience to whom you are speaking – including the interviewer himself. Make sure you convey that message: do not be thrown off track, keep cool, avoid too much gesturing (which the camera will exaggerate), look the interviewer in the eye, speak slowly and clearly, do your best to answer legitimate questions (and do so with your first sentence, before you start explaining), and know when to stop.

In Chapter 13, we looked at public diplomacy campaigns. All campaigns are different, but the essential ingredient for success is luck. Thorough preparation can, however, reduce the risk of failure. Essential questions to ask before designing a campaign are:

i.   What is the strategic aim? What are the objectives we must achieve in support of that aim, and in what time frame?
ii.   Who (and where) are the audience?
iii.   Are we "messaging" or "listening"?
iv.   What resources are at our disposal? Who can we partner with?
v.   Which media channels shall we employ? And which tools and techniques?
vi.   How can we optimise timetabling?
vii.   How shall we evaluate success?
viii.   What are the risks?

Looking at case studies of past campaigns, we observed that the successes variously featured, *inter alia*, sound policies, listening research, limited objectives, careful audience selection, well-crafted youth exchanges and advocacy by third parties. In the failures, the most common misconception was that appearance and reality could be two different things without the audience noticing. This last point reminded us that no public diplomacy campaign can perform miracles: it will have no positive influence if it does not accord with your government's actual policies or the facts on the ground.

The final chapter in Part 2, Chapter 14, considered evaluation. There are many problems associated with evaluation, including the difficulty of attribution in measuring long-term success and the intangibility of what is being measured. Evaluation is also costly, but the benefits are also many, including better allocation of resources and development of best practice. Evaluation is in any case unavoidable if budgets are to be justified.

We saw that successful evaluation included inter alia leadership buy-in, a systematic approach with a strategic plan, independent evaluations, measurable objectives connected to the organisational mission, training, actionable data, stakeholder involvement, adequate resources and audience research. Much evaluation focuses on programmes, because this is easier and cheaper and (and required by funders). Cross-cutting evaluation, while more difficult, can produce additional efficiencies. Other approaches include systems analysis (which treats all public diplomacy activities as a single programme), frame-based assessment and network analysis.

The two basic approaches to evaluation are to analyse the process (i.e. how efficiently a programme is working) or – far more difficult and time-consuming – the impact (i.e. what the actual results are). Another choice is to be made between quantitative analysis and more resource-intensive qualitative analysis (which are most effective when combined). Measurement of inputs and outputs is relatively easy. Measuring outcomes, particularly long-term outcomes, is much more difficult.

We observed that polling is a long-standing tool of public diplomacy evaluation, but that many polls are too general to permit precise attribution, for which focus groups and interviews are necessary. Digital technologies have greatly facilitated the collation and analysis of evaluation data. Increasingly sophisticated software is also beginning to help governments assess the value of their own activities in the digital world.

Confident measurement of long-term public diplomacy outcomes remains the Holy Grail. In the meantime, improved measurement of intermediate outcomes provides helpful signals about the long term.

15.3 Key lessons

Readers of this book should by now have an understanding of the nature of public diplomacy and knowledge of the tools and techniques involved in its practice.

What are the key principles that public diplomacy practitioners should always bear in mind? Dr Nicholas Cull, Professor of Public Diplomacy at the University of Southern California, offers seven lessons, drawn from recent history, which provide an excellent basis for discussion of this question.[170] Readers will recognise these seven principles, to all of which reference has been made at some point during this course.

15.4 Cull's seven lessons

Cull argues as follows:

(1) Public Diplomacy begins with listening.

Cull observes that, for most governments, the first thought is to speak. But before speaking you need to listen, and systematically collect and analyse the opinions of foreign publics. You also need to be seen by your target audience to be genuinely listening.

Comment: We have already observed that, while listening alone may not exert much influence (although sometimes it can), it is an absolute pre-requisite for getting your message right.

---

170   Nicholas J. Cull, *Public Diplomacy: Seven lessons for its Future from its Past*, Place Branding and Public Diplomacy, 2010, Volume 6, Number 1, pp. 11-17 : http://www.palgrave-journals.com/pb/journal/v6/n1/abs/pb20104a.html#top (Abstract only) (Retrieved August 2015).

(2) Public Diplomacy must be connected to policy.

What counts is not what you say but what you do: there is no substitute for sound policy. Cull also stresses the importance of the link between listening and policy-making, while cautioning that sound policies on their own will make no difference to a nation's influence if they are not publicised or coordinated with public diplomacy: the latter must become an integral part of policy-making and delivery.

<u>Comment</u>: This is a central tenet of this course: no amount of public diplomacy, however brilliant, can hope to repair the damage done by fundamentally bad policies.

(3) Public Diplomacy is not a performance for domestic consumption.

Cull's point here is that one should not confuse public diplomacy, which is aimed at overseas audiences, with "domestic socialisation", which seeks to bring domestic constituencies in line with governments' policies.

<u>Comment</u>: This is logically correct and is reflected in the organisational structures of most governments. In the information age, however, as barriers between domestic and foreign policies dissolve, it is becoming progressively more difficult to speak differently to audiences at home and overseas.

(4) Effective public diplomacy requires credibility, but that has implications for the bureaucratic structure around the activity.

The problem is that credibility rests on different foundations in different circumstances:

i.   In listening and advocacy, credibility stems from closeness to the sources of foreign policy (implying authority, and ability to influence);
ii. In broadcasting, credibility derives from adherence to a journalistic ethos and independence of view;
iii. In cultural relations, including educational exchange programmes, there is no overt message; credibility is therefore maximised by distance from government.

<u>Comment</u>: As we have observed, these varying criteria for credibility frequently give rise to tensions between those advocating independent action and those insisting on policy coordination. Sometimes this tension can be creatively managed through construction of sensibly designed institutions.[171]

(5) Sometimes the most credible voice is not one's own.

Cull offers the example of efforts to influence European publics about deployment of Intermediate-Range Nuclear Forces (INF) in the 1980s, when the US Ambassador to NATO worked through regional opinion makers (journalists, think-tankers, etc.).

<u>Comment</u>: As we have seen, this is a basic precept of advertising and public relations. Cull's example (which has been quoted elsewhere in this book) provides powerful support for his argument.

---

171   In the United Kingdom, for example, this tension is constructively managed by virtue of the fact that the BBC and the British Council operate at arm's length from government and thus preserve the credibility of autonomy.

(6) Sometimes Public Diplomacy is not about "you".

Public Diplomacy may be aimed at engineering a general improvement of the international environment or empowering indigenous voices in target countries.[172]

Comment: This is undoubtedly a valuable lesson for public diplomacy practitioners in developed or rapidly emerging economies. Developing countries may regard it as something of a luxury.

(7) Public Diplomacy is everyone's business.

Cull offers as a positive example of this lesson the success of town-twinning in effecting reconciliation between France and Germany after the Second World War. He also points out the damage that can be caused to a country's public diplomacy by the errant behaviour of individual citizens.

Comment: Here a pernickety professional diplomat might part company with Cull, arguing that diplomacy, public or otherwise, is a function of states, even though – as is undeniably the case – states are obliged to collaborate with a range of non-state actors to achieve their ends (which can also be confounded by the bad behaviour of their citizens). There is little argument, however, that nation branding is everyone's business, given the impact of the actions of all – for instance, tourists or immigration officials – who come into contact with the target audiences.

15.5 Conclusions

This book has sought to demonstrate the complexity of public diplomacy, and the difficulty of evaluating its results, but also to offer guidance on how to practise it effectively. There are many options for public diplomacy activity open to governments. These options are being progressively enhanced by digital technologies, although face-to-face contact remains the most effective mode of communication. Circumstances, not least the available resources, will largely determine the particular form of public diplomacy that different governments adopt. In all cases, however, they will be wise to bear Cull's lessons in mind – and, if nothing else, to listen before they speak and to ensure that their public diplomacy is grounded in sound policies.

The final chapter in this book will discuss human resources and training.

---

172   Cull points to the example of the Wilton Park Conference Centre, "a zone for free international exchange of views on key issues of the day". These issues may have nothing to do with the United Kingdom directly.

Chapter 16

Human Resources and Training Needs

16.1 Introduction
16.2 Human resources
16.3 Training

Participants at the Leadership Workshop for WMO Delegates, 2015
UNITAR/Lorenzo Franchi

16.1 Introduction

Now that we have examined public diplomacy, and how it can be practised, it is time to turn our attention, in this final chapter, to the implications for human resources and training.

16.2 Human resources

Harold Nicolson once famously listed his personal choice of attributes for a diplomat as follows:

> "These, then, are the qualities of my ideal diplomatist. Truth, accuracy, calm, patience, good temper, modesty and loyalty. They are also the qualities of an ideal diplomacy. But, the reader may object, you have forgotten intelligence, knowledge, discernment, prudence, hospitality, charm, industry, courage and even tact. I have not forgotten them. I have taken them for granted." [173]

To a 21st Century reader, this list may seem rather quaint. We expect diplomats today to demonstrate rather more technical prowess: understanding of politics, economics and law, and mastery of a range of difficult cross-cutting issues such as climate change, human rights and international security. And yet many of Nicolson's requirements – not least truth, accuracy, discernment, prudence and tact – are precisely those that need to be deployed in successful public diplomacy, translating, as they do, into a willingness and capacity to listen to others, and to engage honestly in dialogue with them.

This raises the question as to whether it makes sense to create a separate cadre for public diplomacy practitioners, who will focus on public diplomacy throughout their careers. Or should the work be left to mainstream diplomatic officers, who will come from, and in due course return to, other diplomatic work? In those cases where separate publicly funded institutions manage, for example, cultural relations[174], governments have taken a clear decision that this particular activity should be conducted with a degree of autonomy by staff in a separate career structure from that of mainstream diplomats. The same may be said of broadcasting institutions, although the extent of editorial independence of these institutions varies considerably. There are also technical tasks, such as website management or video-making, that call for specialist expertise, whether in-house or contracted out. But what about policy advocacy or news management, which are indisputably a function of foreign ministries?

There is no single answer to this question, and much will depend on the traditions of particular diplomatic services.[175] In one sense, public diplomacy is the business of all diplomats, since none are immune to the pressures of the information age and the need to take media and public reaction into account when formulating, and executing, policy. But is everyone equally equipped to deploy the tools and techniques required for public diplomacy?

---

173   Harold Nicolson, *Diplomacy*, San Diego, Harcourt Brace, 1939.
174   Obvious examples are the Alliance Française, the Goethe Institute, the British Council and the Confucius Centres. In the United States, however, the once separate United States Information Agency (USIA) has been folded into the State Department.
175   There is some similarity here with the different ways in which trade and investment promotion is managed by different countries. For example, the British trade and investment promotion body UKTI is staffed in large part by diplomats, and its overseas activities fully integrated into the work of embassies. Many other countries (e.g. Australia, Norway and Japan) operate through autonomous agencies with separate overseas offices.

The danger in generalist diplomats practising public diplomacy is that they may seem like dilettantes to those with whom they interact in the media and civil society. The danger for full-time public diplomacy specialists, on the other hand, is that they may become divorced from the policy process and therefore less well placed to speak authoritatively. (For smaller diplomatic services a separate cadre for public diplomacy practitioners is, in any case, an undreamt of luxury.) One way of managing this dilemma is for a proportion of mainstream diplomats to have public diplomacy as their career anchor, thus permitting them to develop expertise through returning regularly to public diplomacy postings in between work in other areas. Another is to contract people with, for example, media experience to fill particular public diplomacy slots working alongside generalist diplomats. Inevitably there will be an element of compromise in any such arrangements. And in all cases, appropriate training is indispensable.

16.3 Training

This book has aimed to introduce participants to public diplomacy and offer some guidance as to how it is practised. There are however obvious limits to what you can learn from a book. What other training would be beneficial?

First and foremost, there is cross-cultural communication. We have observed the importance of listening to, and understanding, your target audience. You cannot do this without knowledge of the geography, history, language, politics, economics and culture of the people you are seeking to influence. There are generic courses in cross-cultural communication. And we have looked briefly in this book at communication theory, which would bear further study. But, given the particularity of individual cultures, much of the required understanding will come from private study and, in due course, direct exposure to the societies concerned. Language tuition is however indispensable to the process.

Then comes training in the tools and techniques of public diplomacy. We have looked at these in this course and offered guidance in matters such as speech-making and dealing with the media, including being interviewed. We have also examined the essential elements of a public diplomacy campaign. There is however no substitute for learning by doing. So public diplomacy training should include opportunities for practising speech-making, being interviewed, constructing a media plan and organising a public diplomacy campaign. The techniques of evaluation should also be addressed. There might also be simulations of, for example, crisis management.

Training will also be necessary to generate familiarity with the administration of particular national programmes in fields such as educational exchanges and visitor programmes.[176]

Given the growing significance of digital technologies, a special mention needs to be made of IT training. In one sense, such training is scarcely necessary: the current generation of young diplomats has been born into the digital age and has naturally imbibed the relevant technologies. On the other hand, there are particular skills in which people can be trained.

---

176   As an illustration, see for example the public diplomacy training programme of the US State Department: http://fsitraining.state.gov/Docs/FSI_Course_Catalog.pdf (Retrieved August 2015).

For example, a recent workshop run by the DiploFoundation argued that diplomats in the information age needed to be trained to:

    i.   Curate – to find, filter and collate information;
    ii.   Critique – to assess the validity of information and the authenticity of the source;
    iii.   Create – to write weblogs, to store and manage information in new ways;
    iv.   Communicate – to connect with others, to distribute information; and
    v.   Collaborate – to work with others, to share ideas, to build co-operation.[177]

Finally, there is the overarching issue of project management. By and large, diplomats are not well prepared for this, their natural strengths residing in intellectual tasks such as analysis and policy advice or interpersonal activities such as negotiating and lobbying. It should however be evident from the lessons on public diplomacy campaigns that these are, in fact, projects and would derive benefit from being managed as such. Training in at least the essentials of project management would therefore be advisable.

One last word. Valuable – and indeed indispensable – as training may be, the experience of actually doing the job is what creates a truly successful public diplomacy practitioner. Making speeches, being interviewed, briefing the press or participating in a real public diplomacy campaign will feel very different from training exercises and teach you far more valuables lessons. Training will help you talk the walk. In real life you have to walk the walk.

---

177   See the report of the International Forum on Diplomatic Training at the 38th Meeting of Deans and Directors of Diplomatic Academies and Institutes of International Relations, Malta, 27 – 29 September 2010: http://forum.diplomacy.edu/.

Further Reading

View of the Secretariat (left) and Dag Hammarskjöld
Library buildings at UN Headquarters
UN Photo/JC McIlwaine

Recommended reading

Cull, Nicolas J., *Public Diplomacy: Lessons from the Past*, CDC Perspectives on Public Diplomacy, US Center on Public Diplomacy at the Annenberg School, University of Southern California, 2009: http://uscpublicdiplomacy.org/publications/perspectives/CPDPerspectivesLessons.pdf (Retrieved August 2015).

Melissen, Jan, *The New Public Diplomacy: Soft Power in International Relations*, Palgrave Macmillan, 2005: http://kimo-mp3.at.ua/_ld/0/87_en-09.pdf (Retrieved August 2015).

Nye, Joseph S., *Soft Power: The Means to Success in World Politics*, New York, Public Affairs, 2004, especially pp. 1-32 & 99-125.

Rolfe, Mark, *Rhetorical Traditions of Public Diplomacy and the Internet*, The Hague Journal of Diplomacy, 2014, Volume 9, Number 1, pp. 76-83 & 94-101.

Westcott, Nicholas, *Digital Diplomacy: The Impact of the Internet on International Relations*, OII Working Paper, Number 16, Oxford Internet Institute, 16 July 2008: http://ssrn.com/abstract=1326476 (Retrieved August 2015).

Further reading

Anholt, Simon, *Nation 'Branding': Propaganda or Statecraft?*, Public Diplomacy Magazine, Los Angeles, University of Southern California, Summer 2009, Issue 2: http://www.simonanholt.com/Publications/publications-other-articles.aspx (Retrieved August 2015).

Banks, Robert, *A Resource Guide to Public Diplomacy Evaluation*, Los Angeles, Figueroa Press, 2011: http://uscpublicdiplomacy.org/publications/perspectives/CPD_Perspectives_Paper%209_2011.pdf (Retrieved August 2015).

Cull, Nicholas J., *Public Diplomacy: Seven lessons for its Future from its Past*, Place Branding and Public Diplomacy, 2010, Volume 6, Number 1, pp. 11-17 : http://www.palgrave-journals.com/pb/journal/v6/n1/abs/pb20104a.html#top (abstract only) (Retrieved August 2015).

Dainton, Marianne & Zelley, Elaine D., *Applying Communication Theory for Professional Life: A Practical Introduction*, London, Sage Publications Inc., 2nd edition, 2011.

Fisher, Ali & Aurélie Bröckerhoff, *Options for Influence: Global Campaigns of Persuasion in the New Worlds of Public Diplomacy*, London, Counterpoint, 2008: http://www.wandrenpd.com/wp-content/uploads/2011/12/OptionsforInfluence.pdf (Retrieved August 2015).

Henrikson, Alan K., *What Can Public Diplomacy Achieve?*, Discussion Papers in Diplomacy, The Hague, Netherlands Institute of International Relations "Clingendael", 2006, especially pp. 37-38: http://www.peacepalacelibrary.nl/ebooks/files/Clingendael_20060900_cdsp_paper_dip_c.pdf (Retrieved August 2015).

Khatib, Lina, William Dutton & Michael Thelwall, *Public Diplomacy 2.0: An Exploratory Case Study of the US Digital Outreach Team*, CDDRL Working Papers, 120, Stanford, Freeman Spogli Institute for International Studies, January 2011: http://iis-db.stanford.edu/pubs/23084/No.120-_Public_Diplomacy_2.0.pdf (Retrieved August 2015).

McClory, Jonathan, *The New Persuaders III: A 2012 Global Ranking of Soft Power*, London, Institute for Government, December 2012: http://www.instituteforgovernment.org.uk/sites/default/files/publications/The%20new%20persuaders%20III_0.pdf (Retrieved August 2015).

Melissen, Jan, *Beyond the New Public Diplomacy*, The Hague, Netherlands Institute of International Relations "Clingendael", 2011, Number 3 : http://www.clingendael.nl/publications/2011/20111014_cdsp_paper_jmelissen.pdf

O'Halloran, Richard, *Strategic Communication*, Parameters, Carlisle, US Army War College, Autumn 2007, pp. 4-14: http://strategicstudiesinstitute.army.mil/pubs/parameters/Articles/07autumn/halloran.pdf (Retrieved August 2015).

Pamment, James, *What Became of the New Public Diplomacy? Recent Developments in British, US and Swedish Public Diplomacy Policy and Evaluation Methods*, The Hague Journal of Diplomacy, 2012, Volume 7, Number 3, pp. 313-336.